In Defense of the Economic
Analysis of Regulation

In Defense of the Economic Analysis of Regulation

Robert W. Hahn

AEI-Brookings Joint Center for Regulatory Studies

WASHINGTON, D.C.

Available in the United States from the AEI Press, c/o Client Distribution Services, 193 Edwards Drive, Jackson, TN 38301. To order, call toll free: 1-800-343-4499. Distributed outside the United States by arrangement with Eurospan, 3 Henrietta Street, London WC2E 8LU, England.

Library of Congress Cataloging-in-Publication Data

Hahn, Robert William.
    In defense of the economic analysis of regulation / Robert W. Hahn.
        p. cm.
    "A shorter version of this piece appeared in the University of Chicago Law Review"—Acknowledgments
    Includes bibliographical references.
    ISBN 0-8447-7186-4 (pbk. : alk. paper)
    1. Law—Economic aspects—United States. 2. Law—United States—Decision making—Cost effectiveness. 3. Cost effectiveness. I. Title.

    K487.E3H34 2005
    320.6'072—dc22

                                                        2004029300

10 09 08 07 06 05   1 2 3 4 5

American Enterprise Institute
1150 17th Street, N.W.
Washington, D.C. 20036

Printed in the United States of America

Contents

Illustrations

Foreword

This volume is one in a series commissioned by the AEI-Brookings Joint Center for Regulatory Studies to contribute to the continuing debate over regulatory reform. The series addresses several fundamental issues in regulation, including the design of effective reforms, the impact of proposed reforms on the public, and the political and institutional forces that affect reform.

Many forms of regulation have grown dramatically in recent decades—especially in the areas of environment, health, and safety. Moreover, expenditures in those areas are likely to continue to grow faster than the rate of government spending. Yet, the economic impact of regulation receives much less scrutiny than direct, budgeted government spending. We believe that policymakers need to rectify that imbalance.

In this volume, Robert W. Hahn offers a defense of the economic analysis of regulation. He addresses a number of criticisms raised by a group of legal scholars who argue that such analysis is generally flawed and misleading. He shows how economic analysis has made important contributions to our understanding of the federal regulatory process, and suggests how analysis can better inform policy discussions.

Like all Joint Center publications, this monograph can be freely downloaded at www.aei-brookings.org. We encourage educators to distribute these materials to their students.

ROBERT W. HAHN, Executive Director
ROBERT E. LITAN, Director
AEI-Brookings Joint Center for Regulatory Studies

Acknowledgments

A shorter version of this piece appeared in the *University of Chicago Law Review*. I would like to thank Maureen Cropper, Scott Farrow, Bill Ferranti, Randall Kroszner, Alan Krupnick, Lester Lave, Robert Litan, Randall Lutter, Al McGartland, John Morrall, Eric Posner, Cass Sunstein, Scott Wallsten, and Jonathan Wiener for helpful comments and Rohit Malik and Patrick Dudley for excellent research assistance. I am solely responsible for the views expressed in this monograph.

In Defense of the Economic Analysis of Regulation

Robert W. Hahn

I

INTRODUCTION

Over the past several decades, there have been numerous critiques of the application of economic approaches to problems in public policy.[1] Indeed, several books and articles criticize various aspects of cost-benefit analysis and economic policy analysis more generally.[2] There have also been a number of defenses of quantitative approaches to analyzing important public policy issues.[3] For example, Professor Sunstein, in *Risk and Reason*, argues for an approach that would weigh the costs and benefits of different policies but also consider a number of other factors.[4] And Justice Breyer argues that government needs to set regulatory priorities differently, so that more lives can be saved for a given amount of money.[5]

The debate over the use of economic analysis as a tool in regulatory decision making has been more than academic. Countries and states throughout the world require extensive use of cost-benefit analysis and related tools as a way of informing key regulatory decisions and reforming the regulatory process. In the United States, for example, the regulatory oversight agency uses cost-benefit

1

analysis to both improve regulatory proposals and stimulate new regulatory measures where the benefits exceed the costs.[6]

Scholars generally agree that economic analysis is becoming a more important part of regulatory decision making. Sunstein argues that we are witnessing the emergence of a "cost-benefit state" in the United States.[7] Other scholars have argued that the trend extends around the world.[8] The issue is not simply which analysts are right in analyzing a particular regulation, but how responsible governments should make multimillion- and billion-dollar decisions that affect their citizens.

Recently, the application of economic approaches to problems in regulation has created a veritable firestorm in some parts of the legal community.[9] The debate has been particularly strident in the area of environmental, health, and safety regulation.[10] According to government estimates, the costs associated with this regulation are substantial—on the order of $200 billion annually.[11] The benefits, which are harder to pin down, may be even larger.[12] Thus, changes in the regulatory apparatus can significantly affect the public's health and welfare.

Supporters of the use of economic analysis in measuring regulatory impacts agree that placing monetary values on the costs and benefits of regulation is difficult.[13] The critics, however, argue that the techniques of economic analysis and their applications are fundamentally flawed.[14]

One particularly controversial approach that scholars have used to gain insight into the general impact of regulation is the use of scorecards. Scorecards typically attempt to summarize the impact of different regulations based on a number of indicators.[15] Examples of these indicators include costs, benefits, cost savings, lives or life-years saved, cost-effectiveness, and net benefits.[16] For example, in an important early paper, Morrall developed an analysis that suggested that the cost-effectiveness of regulation (measured by the cost per life saved) varied over several orders of magnitude.[17] More recent work by Tengs and others amplifies on that theme, arguing that there are often important differences in the cost-effectiveness of life-saving interventions.[18]

Differences in the cost-effectiveness of different investments in life-saving activities could have important implications for public policy. It matters, in terms of the number of lives likely to be saved,[19] whether the government mandates reductions in radiation exposure on X-ray equipment ($23,000 per life-year saved) or radiation emission controls at uranium fuel cycle facilities ($34 billion per life-year saved) or when the government institutes a mandatory seat belt use law ($69 per life-year saved) versus requiring airbag installation in cars ($120,000 per life-year saved).[20] In some cases, the government can and does advocate several different life-saving investments.[21] But, because such investments are frequently expensive and resources are limited, there is a need to prioritize.[22] Tengs and Graham illustrate the possible gains from prioritizing expenditures. They show that changing the mix of life-saving investments has the potential to save thousands of additional lives at no additional cost.[23]

In related work, I assembled and analyzed the most comprehensive set of federal regulations to date.[24] Using the government's numbers contained in regulatory analyses, I found results similar to Tengs, Graham, and Morrall. Cost-effectiveness varied over several orders of magnitude. In a calculation similar to Tengs and Graham, I argued that reallocating funding to life-saving alternatives in developing countries could save substantially more lives at the same or lower cost.[25] In addition, I found that the total benefits associated with the regulations examined exceeded the total costs. Perhaps my most controversial finding, at least the one hardest for the critics to accept, was that a substantial number of regulations would not pass an economist's strict benefit-cost test based on the government's numbers.[26]

In a recent paper, Parker argues that the regulatory scorecards used by me and others are deeply flawed and should be abandoned.[27] He analyzes the work of Morrall, Tengs, Graham, myself, and others, arguing that it has serious deficiencies. In this monograph, I respond to those criticisms. My objectives in this monograph are more ambitious than that, however; this monograph also examines some general critiques of the economic analysis of social regulation.[28] While the arguments advanced by some of the critics have some validity, by and large, the analysis they find so offensive has yielded important research and policy insights and has also led to more efficient regulation. The solution to legitimate concerns raised by the critics is not to eliminate the quantitative analysis but to gain a deeper understanding of its strengths and weaknesses and use it wisely.

This monograph is organized as follows: Section II provides a review of the main critiques found in the legal literature aimed at the alleged misuse or abuse of regulatory scorecards and economics in assessing the impact of environmental, health, and safety regulation. Section III responds to critics of my work and provides a comprehensive examination of the government's regulatory impact assessments. I specifically respond to many of the criticisms offered by Parker and his colleagues.[29] Section IV identifies some of the key contributions that regulatory scorecards and economic analysis have made to our understanding of policies and regulations aimed at improving environment, health, and safety. Section V identifies areas where the critics of economic analysis of regulation and I seem to agree, at least in part. Finally, section VI concludes.

II

A Review of the Main Critiques

In this section, I summarize many major criticisms of scorecards and related work that have been made by a group of legal scholars I refer to as the "critics." Major critics include McGarity, Heinzerling, and more recently, Parker.[30] Many of these critics participate in a recently formed group called the Center for Progressive Regulation, which provides some background on their perspective.[31]

I primarily consider critiques of five papers, which I call the *main studies* for ease of exposition. They include (1) a paper by

Morrall that presents a famous table on the cost-effectiveness of regulations measured in cost per life saved; (2) a paper by Tengs et al. that examines the cost-effectiveness of life-saving interventions in the United States from publicly available economic analyses; (3) a paper by Tengs and Graham that uses the data from Tengs et al. to assess the opportunity costs of social investments in life-saving; and (4 and 5) two studies by Hahn that assemble information on the costs and benefits of regulation using government regulatory impact analyses (RIAs) as the basis for analysis.[32] These studies have been critiqued by a number of the critics, including Heinzerling, Parker, Ackerman, Shapiro, and Glicksman.[33]

According to Parker, the thread that ties together these main studies is that they are influential studies that used regulatory scorecards to characterize regulation. But, what is a regulatory scorecard? I define a scorecard more broadly than Parker, who considers primarily summary statistics on the net benefits and cost-effectiveness of regulations.[34] He evidently views scorecards as the "leading source of regulatory skepticism" and the main source for the "remarkable ascendancy of the anti-regulatory movement."[35] Parker also assumes that researchers creating scorecards claim that rule analyses are final declarations of costs and benefits.[36] This characterization is unduly narrow and incorrect, even in light of the papers he critiques. Scorecards are not simply summary statistics and are neither antiregulatory tools nor final declarations.[37] Moreover, as shown later, scorecards can reveal weaknesses in an agency's analysis and potential areas for improvement.[38]

A scorecard could be either an accounting framework or a description of summary statistics that helps shed light on the measurement of the costs, benefits, or costs and benefits of a regulation or several regulations. Thus, a scorecard need not be a table or a scorecard in the traditional sense, although it could. For example, Freeman provides summary statistics on the costs and benefits of environmental regulation.[39] Hopkins provides an influential summary table on the costs of regulation.[40] Hahn and Hird do a study on the costs and benefits of regulation with tables that tally up benefits and costs.[41] And Hahn and Sunstein offer a scorecard for individual regulations so that government and citizens can get information more easily about the impact of regulations.[42]

The point is that scorecards of regulatory activity come in many shapes and sizes. Scorecards consider a range of output measures, including net benefits and quality indicators, such as whether an RIA quantitatively assessed alternatives and included certain information in its executive summary. The critics focus on those scorecards that include measures of cost and benefits that are not to their liking because they suggest that a significant number of regulations fail a cost-benefit test. They also focus on measures of cost-effectiveness that they feel are lacking in some way.[43]

Many of the analyses of scorecards offered by the critics would have the substantive effect of making regulations look more favorable in the light of a cost-benefit test. I consider six general critiques next.

Discounting of Benefits Is Wrong and Antiregulatory

The discount rate is critical in cost-benefit analysis. Economists use discounting to make costs and benefits that occur in different time periods comparable. The basic rationale for discounting is that consumers are not indifferent between consuming a dollar's worth of a good today and one dollar, say, next year.[44] In general, if given a choice, a consumer would require something more than one dollar next year in exchange for giving up one dollar today. So, for example, a consumer may invest a dollar in a money market account or bond today in the hopes of getting more than a dollar a year from now.

Economists generally agree that some kind of discounting is necessary to take this rate of time preference into account. There is some disagreement on the appropriate rate at which to discount and whether this rate should be constant or vary with time.[45] In practice, most cost-benefit analysts use a constant rate. There is also disagreement about the appropriate basis for selecting the rate.

The critics generally suggest using lower discount rates than are typically used in practice. Their recommendations would generally have the effect of raising the level of benefits in comparison to costs, thus making regulation look more favorable than it otherwise would. The reason that lower discount rates tend to increase net benefits is that benefits, such as lives saved,[46] typically occur later in time than the major portion of costs, which are often some upfront investments in equipment or products. Therefore, when one uses a higher discount rate, the benefits get discounted more heavily relative to the costs.[47]

Some of the critics argue that the discount rates used in cost-benefit analysis are too high. Parker, for example, objects to my choice of 5 percent in my base-case analysis of regulations with a range of 3–7 percent.[48] He suggests that the range should be 2–3 percent.[49]

Unfortunately, there is no unanimous agreement on the correct choice for a discount rate.[50] However, there is a great deal of support in practice for the range of numbers I used. Economic guidance issued by the Office of Management and Budget during the Clinton administration recommended a discount rate of 7 percent.[51] Guidance from the Office of Management and Budget (OMB) during the George W. Bush administration suggests that rates between 3 and 7 percent are best.[52]

Some critics would go further, arguing that discounting at all is wrong for environmental and health policies.[53] Surprisingly, some of the authors even concede an inherent bias in their calculations, stating, "Our approach, according to the conventional methodology, would overstate benefits."[54]

Not discounting lives or benefit streams creates several problems. If lives are not discounted, it essentially means that a policy planner is indifferent between a life saved today and a life saved tomorrow. That would mean that if costs were discounted at some positive rate, it would pay to defer investments in life-saving indefinitely.[55] The reason is that the discounted costs would be lower if they are deferred, but the discounted benefits would be the same. In the extreme, if it cost a dollar to save a life today or 1,000 years from now, the planner would always opt to save the life 1,000 years from now, which is a curious result.[56]

In short, the critics' case for not discounting is not persuasive or compelling.[57] Moreover, using a discount rate to discount future benefits and costs is justified and widely accepted.[58]

The critique of the range I chose in the study discussed below is not compelling, either.[59] It is a reasonable range based on our understanding of economics and fully supported by guidelines of the OMB during the last eight years.

Selection Bias Is Generally Antiregulatory

The critics claim that some scorecards have a bias against promoting additional regulations that could be socially beneficial. In particular, they suggest that a selection bias in certain scorecards excludes possible new or existing regulations that are likely to be cost-effective or pass a cost-benefit test.[60]

Unfortunately, virtually all empirical studies of complex social phenomena have some kind of selection bias. The key questions to ask are whether the selection bias is likely to dramatically change the nature of the conclusions reached, and whether the study could help contribute to knowledge that would address important selection biases in the future. Here, I consider the issue of contributions to knowledge.[61]

The historical context in which scholarship is done is important. Empirical scholars tend to focus on areas where they can obtain data. Thus, even if there were a selection bias in the studies examined by the critics, this line of research has made important contributions and will continue to help overcome the selection biases identified by the critics. Consider Morrall's table on differences in cost-effectiveness among regulations. Prior to his table in "A Review of the Record," no systematic database on the cost-effectiveness of federal regulations existed, to my knowledge. So, even if important potential or final regulations were missing, this database serves as a basis for developing the knowledge base needed to address the concerns raised by the critics.

Morrall's research provides a good illustration of how initial research can evolve over time. In a recent draft paper that responds persuasively to Heinzerling, Morrall shows that there are, indeed, new regulatory opportunities that are likely to be attractive.[62] Moreover, the agency where he works, the OMB, recently was at the forefront of identifying potential regulatory opportunities that are either efficient or cost-effective.[63]

The same argument can be applied to the research by Tengs et al. and Hahn. Tengs et al. is the most ambitious attempt I know of to systematize the cost-effectiveness of regulations and other life-saving interventions in the United States.[64] Similarly, my studies reflect an attempt to systematize knowledge on regulatory impact analyses.[65] Yet, Parker, for example, criticizes my work for focusing only on so-called major rules, or significant regulatory actions. He asserts that proposed or actual minor rules would have been more cost effective and thus there is an "in-built sampling bias against regulation" in my data.[66] Unfortunately, we do not know whether minor rules would have been more cost-effective because the data are not yet available to analyze this problem.[67] In the case of minor rules, we cannot say, for example, that they are better on average than major rules. While Parker thinks they are,[68] he presents no evidence. Minor rules are not subject to the same level of scrutiny as major rules by the OMB. Thus, there is less incentive for an agency to pay attention to costs and net benefits of a regulation than it might for major rules.[69] Significantly, regulatory agencies often prefer their rules not to be major so that they do not have to undergo White House review. Indeed, agencies have been known to package some of their rules so as to avoid significant regulatory oversight. Thus, the selection bias in my work might tilt toward more, not less, cost-effective regulation.[70]

Another potential bias arises because agencies may tend to overstate benefits and understate costs to make their regulations pass benefit-cost tests and OMB reviews. This type of bias, ignored by the critics, would be pro-regulatory, not antiregulatory. Justice Breyer, for example, characterizes agencies as having "tunnel vision, a 'classic administrative disease' [that] arises when an agency so organizes or subdivides its tasks that each employee's individual conscientious performance effectively carries single-minded pursuit of a single goal too far, to the point where it brings about more harm than good."[71]

"Tunnel vision" not only drives agencies to go the last, costly mile, but it can also cause them to defend their regulations by reporting additional benefits and ignoring incremental costs.

In summary, selection bias is a problem in these studies, but it is a problem in virtually all studies like these. Moreover, the selection bias may not run entirely in the direction that the critics suggest. While I concede that some interventions not considered by the main studies are likely to have been economic winners, many other regulations and interventions not considered are likely to have been economic losers.

Use of Ex-Ante Estimates May Be Antiregulatory

The complexity of the real world makes any empirical work difficult. One of the ways that regulatory scholars and regulators deal with the complexity is to estimate the costs and benefits of a regulation *before* it is actually implemented, so-called ex-ante estimates. All the main studies addressed by the critics, for example, use "ex-ante" measures of costs and benefits. Some of the critics have argued that ex-ante measures may be misleading because, for example, they may overstate actual costs.

The critics assert that this is a big problem because the actual net benefits of a policy could differ markedly from those estimated before the policy is put in place. While this is true, policymakers do not have a measure of ex-post costs and benefits available when policies are actually implemented.[72]

Potential problems with the use of ex-ante costs have been recognized for some time.[73] Indeed, I pointed it out in an early study that has been analyzed by the critics.[74] Moreover, all the main studies reveal that they are based on estimated ex-ante data, even if the term *ex ante* is not used.[75] But the critics assert that this problem is a fundamental flaw of the main studies.[76] Whether they are right depends on your frame of reference.

In the best of all worlds, we would prefer to know the "truth" on benefits and costs, assuming "truth" exists. The next best alternative might be to have an unbiased estimate of the economic impact of a regulation as it was implemented.[77] The next best after that might be to have an unbiased estimate of the economic impact of a regulation before it is implemented. And far behind that would be to have no estimate at all.

Herein lies the problem. There are few studies on the retrospective impact of regulations, particularly for the regulations reviewed in the main studies. Thus, we are left with the problem of what to use in place of ex-ante estimates. The answer is not obvious. One could adjust those estimates in some systematic ways, but in my opinion, we have insufficient information to do so now.[78] Furthermore, some scholars found that ex-ante estimates may overstate benefits as frequently as costs.[79]

Thus, the potential ex-ante problem may not be nearly as perverse as the critics suggest. And there is no obvious alternative at this point. I believe, in this case, some data on these subjects are better than no data, both for assessing the aggregate impact of regulations within and across programs and the individual impact of regulations. Proposed regulations must be evaluated. By definition, evaluating a proposal is an ex-ante study. Therefore, while I am sympathetic to the concerns raised by the critics, I see no obvious alternative at this juncture.

Quantitative Economic Analysis Is Antiregulatory because It Squeezes Out Qualitative Benefits

There is a general concern that quantitative analysis may dominate important qualitative issues.[80] The critics appear to be concerned primarily with unquantified or unquantifiable benefits.[81]

I am concerned about this issue and think that both qualitative and quantitative factors should be taken into account in regulatory decision making.[82] The critics specifically criticize the main studies for focusing too much on quantitative factors. This criticism is misguided, because the primary purpose of the main studies was not to address key qualitative factors in cost-benefit analysis.[83]

Moreover, in my studies, I accounted for a number of factors other than bottom-line issues related to the number or regulations that pass or fail a cost-benefit test and the overall net benefits. Table 1 reprints a table from the study, labeled "Regulatory Scorecard, 1981 to mid-1996."[84] However, Parker does not mention this scorecard in his critique, which purports to address regulatory scorecards. Instead, he focuses on my scorecard aimed at actually quantifying benefits and costs. One objective of table 1 is to assess the frequency with which different quantitative issues were addressed. The rows labeled "Costs assessed" and "Benefits or cost savings assessed" include actual measures of costs, benefits, and cost savings where we could identify them. The primary purpose of this table was to get a better picture of what the agencies were doing. Moreover, the research motivating this table gave rise to subsequent research using scorecards that addresses both *qualitative* and quantitative aspects of regulation.[85]

Several of the critics identify problems with particular scorecards, but Parker believes these problems are serious enough to call for an end to their use.[86] A key part of Parker's critique hinges on the misconceived notion that such approaches do not permit important qualitative factors to enter the analysis.[87]

Parker's analysis has two problems. First, it ignores the important contributions the main studies and related work have made to our understanding of regulation.[88] Second, it ignores the fact that these and other scorecards can be used to help make the very points about qualitative factors that the critics seem to care so much about. A researcher could, for example, add a column to Morrall's well-known table that specifies important qualitative factors to be considered in reaching a decision.[89]

Heinzerling and Ackerman go further than Parker. They argue that, because cost-benefit analysis is time intensive and resource intensive, it is not "useful to keep cost-benefit analysis around as a kind of regulatory tag-along."[90] However, they present no data to suggest that not doing cost-benefit analysis would improve regulatory outcomes or the regulatory process.[91] And they ignore research suggesting that cost-benefit analyses of regulations have been helpful in certain circumstances.[92]

TABLE 1
REGULATORY SCORECARD, 1981 TO MID-1996
(n = 168)

	Total	CPSC	DOL-Health	DOL-Safety	DOT	EPA	HHS	HUD	USDA
Number of rules	168	1	15	13	13	115	5	2	4
Costs assessed	164	1	15	13	13	111	5	2	4
	98%	100%	100%	100%	100%	97%	100%	100%	100%
Benefits or cost savings assessed	146	1	15	13	13	95	5	2	2
	87%	100%	100%	100%	100%	83%	100%	100%	50%
Benefits monetized	44	1	1	3	4	26	5	2	2
	26%	100%	7%	23%	31%	23%	100%	100%	50%

SOURCE: Robert W. Hahn, *Reviving Regulatory Reform* (Washington D.C.: AEI-Brookings Joint Center, 2000).
NOTES: CPSC: Consumer Product Safety Commission; DOL: Department of Labor; DOT: Department of Transportation; EPA: Environmental Protection Agency; HHS: Department of Health and Human Services; HUD: Department of Housing and Urban Development; and USDA: Department of Agriculture.

In summary, the critics' broad concern that quantitative factors may in some cases receive more importance than they deserve is legitimate.[93] But the scorecards that the critics denigrate are not intrinsically flawed in this regard. Moreover, in the absence of good analysis that highlights quantitative economic and social impacts, decision makers at regulatory agencies are likely to be driven more strongly by more narrow political considerations.[94]

The Results of These Studies Are Not Robust

The critics are skeptical of some of the findings in the main studies and suggest that reanalysis of the data could lead to different conclusions.[95] For example, Heinzerling is critical of some of Morrall's findings on cost effectiveness.[96] Morrall has already addressed the charges by Heinzerling and Parker, where he argues that these critics make numerous errors that could have been corrected by a competent peer review process.[97] In the next section, I address the charges that the critics direct at my studies more fully.

I simply wish to suggest that concerns about robustness should be taken seriously. It is of some interest to know, for example, whether Morrall's finding on variations in cost-effectiveness across regulations is likely to be correct and likely to hold in other regulatory contexts. It is of some interest to know whether my finding on the absence of quantitative measures of benefits is the rule rather than the exception, whether a significant number of federal regulations are unlikely to pass a cost-benefit test, and whether we can save more lives for less money. I think the answer to all these questions is probably yes, but the sense in which these findings are true needs to be addressed carefully. Therefore, the critics raise an important issue by questioning the robustness of the findings associated with the main studies.[98] Unfortunately, they do little to help resolve it.

The Benefits and Costs to Subgroups Are Frequently Overlooked in Practice

The critics correctly point out that cost-benefit analysis, as practiced, frequently glosses over important distributional issues.[99] But there is no reason, in principle, that cost-benefit analysis could not address such equity issues.[100] Moreover, scorecards could easily include such information if it were available. For example, if there were information on the impact of a regulation on different income groups, it might be possible to develop an assessment of whether the regulation hurts or helps low-income groups.

The basic problem, in my experience, is that such information is generally unavailable. When the government has mandated the collection of this information, such as in the case of environmental equity, it has failed to act on the mandate.[101]

Most of the RIAs I reviewed do not collect useful information on the distributional impacts of a regulatory policy.[102] While they could, it would be quite expensive because it is very difficult to obtain good information on the distributional impacts of most social regulations.[103]

Even if such information on distributional impacts of a regulatory policy could be obtained, there is a question as to how much influence it should have in the decision-making process. Some academics have argued that regulation is a rather inefficient means for redistributing resources and that other means, such as tax policy, should be used to address distributional issues.[104]

The bottom line for cost-benefit analysis is that this is an age-old issue.[105] The critics find it useful in pursuing their agenda, so they use it. I do not dismiss distributional concerns lightly, but the answer is to begin gathering data on these issues. Those data and information can then be factored into scorecards.

III

CRITICISMS OF THE GOVERNMENT'S NUMBERS STUDIES

This section reviews criticisms leveled at two of the main studies, addressing what the government regulatory impact analyses reveal about the benefits and costs of regulation. The analysis here suggests that, although the critics raised legitimate concerns, they overstated their case.

Both studies that use the government's numbers try to summarize what is known about the costs and benefits of regulation, taking the government's numbers as the primary source of information.[106] Because the results from the later study are more comprehensive than those of the earlier one, I focus on the later study in this section.[107]

The government's numbers are often the result of incomplete— and sometimes flawed—analysis. Nevertheless, the numbers provided in the RIAs are the only available source of data on which we can base a comprehensive review of major federal regulations.[108] I used those estimates to aggregate the net benefits of regulation, provide information on the quality of regulations, and identify factors that could help explain the variation in regulatory efficiency.[109]

My assessment of the government's numbers yielded several conclusions. (1) Aggregate estimates of agency net benefits based on the government's own numbers are positive. (2) The government can increase the net benefits of regulation. Less than half the rules pass a neutral economist's cost-benefit test. Net benefits would increase substantially if agencies rejected such rules. (3) Net benefits exhibit a wide range, which suggests that a reallocation of regulatory resources could increase the aggregate net benefits of regulation.

On reassessment of these findings several years later, I am still in complete agreement with all these conclusions, except for the statement that, "Less than half the rules pass a neutral economist's cost-benefit test." For that finding, for the reasons discussed next, I suggest a suitable refinement is that a significant fraction of regulations would fail a cost-benefit test; my best estimate is that about half the regulations would pass such a test and half would fail. I group criticisms of the study from the critics, primarily Parker, into three categories: benefits and costs, benefits, and costs.[110] I use sensitivity analyses to address those claims that can be addressed with quantitative analysis.

Benefits and Costs

There are two general critiques of the study related to net benefit calculations. First, standardization may introduce biases that reduce net benefits; second, the treatment of uncertainty is problematic.

Standardization Introduces Biases. The rationale for standardizing assumptions in this study was to create a relatively simple way of comparing benefits and costs across regulations. So, I chose to standardize a number of values, including the discount rate, the value of a statistical life, the value of fixed amounts of emission reductions, and the value of reducing certain injuries.[111]

The standardization generated several critiques. First, Parker suggests that I introduced standardized assumptions, making "numerous adjustments to those numbers—usually in the direction of higher costs and lower benefits."[112] This claim is false and Parker provides no data to support his position.[113] None of the standardization assumptions were made to make my analysis come out in a particular way. Moreover, I did sensitivity analyses on a variety of key variables to see how they affected the results.[114]

Parker also appears confused about my treatment of inflation and my choice of a base year.[115] For example, Parker suggests that I do not account for inflation after 1990. This claim is incorrect. For all years in the analysis, including years after 1990, I converted all dollars to 1995 dollars using the consumer price index.[116] Economists frequently focus on making sure that the dollars in their models are in the same year to avoid comparing "apples and oranges." To address that concern, we usually convert dollars into a constant year. So, for example, if a figure were in 1999 dollars and we wished to convert it to 2000 dollars, and prices went up by 5 percent from 1999 to 2000, then dollars would be increased by 5 percent. The choice of any particular year is arbitrary but has an impact on the results.[117]

An additional wrinkle in this model again seems to have confounded Parker. I needed to choose a base year to make my regulations comparable.[118] He highlights the fact that this choice is "arbitrary." Unfortunately, one has to make many arbitrary choices to get over "apples and oranges" problems, and selecting a base year is one of those. The only alternative is to consider dollar magnitudes for different years without adjusting for either inflation or time. This is problematic because it leads to peculiar economic results akin to not discounting.[119] Suppose, for example, that one regulation had actual net benefits of $100 based on a 1980 implementation date and another regulation had net benefits of $190 based on a 1990 implementation date. These figures are not comparable as presented because one dollar in 1980 does not equal one dollar in 1990. To avoid the problem of comparing "apples and oranges" in terms of their overall net benefits, one needs to look at the two regulations from the same vantage point in time.[120] The selection of a base year or particular vantage point in time, like the choice of a uniform dollar year, can affect the results but not the key conclusions.[121] Varying the base year changes the factor by which one discounts net benefits to their present value, not the sign. If the present value of net benefits is positive for a particular base year, then it will still be positive if that base year is moved forward or backward in time.

Treatment of Uncertainty Could Be Improved. There are two major concerns about uncertainty. First, there is false precision in the reporting of the numbers.[122] Second, the study often uses midpoint estimates to describe the most likely value without considering the range or another value the agency may state as plausible.[123]

In general, the treatment of uncertainty can be improved. The question is how far one needs to go to make a point. I consider additional sensitivity analyses here that directly address this issue.

Parker makes a valid point about false precision. In retrospect, I should have reported fewer significant digits in my findings to better reflect the uncertainty in my results.[124]

Parker's problem with my use of midpoints of provided ranges for best estimates is less persuasive. He suggests that I was mistaken in assigning a midpoint when the agency preferred a higher or lower part of the range.[125] Figure 1, taken from Hahn et al., reveals that only 17 percent of RIAs included both a range and best estimate for quantified benefits.[126] Only 13 percent of the RIAs presented both a best estimate and a range of costs.[127] To compare "apples to apples," I derived best estimates for the ranges by taking the midpoint of the range.

Parker criticizes this practice, using the "Great Lakes Water Quality Guidance" as an example. While that RIA suggests that the EPA expected annual costs to be at the lower end of the range rather than at the upper end, it does not specify a best estimate.[128] Moreover, the RIA mentions additional opportunity costs incurred that we did not include in the net benefits calculation. Inclusion of these costs would have lowered the regulation's net benefits.[129] Using the midpoint for the best estimate is consistent and easy to understand. In addition, taking the midpoint of the range is not inherently biased in either direction.

FIGURE 1
AGENCY ANALYSIS OF MONETIZED BENEFITS

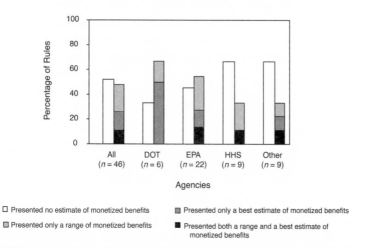

SOURCE: Robert W. Hahn et al., "Assessing Regulatory Impact Analyses: The Failure of Agencies to Comply with Executive Order 12,866," *Harvard Journal of Law and Public Policy* 23, no. 3 (Summer 2000): 869, figure 2.

NOTES: DOT: Department of Transportation; EPA: Environmental Protection Agency; HHS: Health and Human Services; DOC: Department of Commerce; DOE: Department of Energy; DOL: Department of Labor; USDA: Department of Agriculture. The category "Other" includes DOC, DOE, DOL, and USDA.

To account for uncertainty in benefits and costs, I performed a sensitivity analysis using different values for benefits and costs. Table 2 reveals the impact of varying benefits and costs on three cost-benefit measures and illustrates that variations in the estimates of costs and benefits do not affect the key conclusions.[130] In table 2, the discount rate is set at 5 percent and the value of statistical life (VSL) is set at $5 million. The column headings indicate the range of benefits and costs. For example, "high benefits" means that benefits are increased by 25 percent from the base case, and "low costs" means that costs are decreased by 25 percent from the base case. In the first row of the results, the value in each cell is aggregate net benefits for all final regulations; the percentage of final regulations that pass a

TABLE 2

THE IMPACT OF VARYING BENEFITS AND COSTS

$(n = 106)$

	Scenario				
Results	Very low benefits and very high costs	Low bene-fits and high costs	Base case	High bene-fits and low costs	Very high benefits and very low costs
Aggregate net benefits	492	1,134	1,776	2,418	3,062
Percentage that pass a cost-benefit test	38%	40%	43%	44%	48%
Aggregate net benefits of rules that fail a C/B test	−468	−373	−281	−195	−113

SOURCE: Author's calculations.
NOTES: Net benefits are in billions of 1995 dollars. Very low benefits means that benefits are 50 percent of the base case; low benefits means that benefits are 75 percent of the base case; high benefits means that benefits are 125 percent of the base case; very high benefits means that benefits are 150 percent of the base case. The same measures also apply to costs.

cost-benefit test is in the second row; and the aggregate net benefits of final regulations that fail a cost-benefit test are in the third row.

The first row of the table shows that aggregate net benefits remain positive and substantial under all variations of benefits and costs. The second row of the table illustrates that, in all cases, the proportion of final regulations that pass a cost-benefit test is below 50 percent. The third row of the table reveals that the aggregate net benefits for the set of final regulations that fail a cost-benefit test are substantially negative for all ranges of benefits and costs. This result suggests that government can increase the aggregate net benefits of regulations if it rejects rules that fail a cost-benefit test or replaces them with alternatives that pass a cost-benefit test.[131] The table demonstrates that altering the methodology in response to Parker's criticisms does not alter the fundamental conclusions of the analysis.

Analytical Response to Critique on Benefits and Costs. This section provides some quantitative information on the various critiques.

TABLE 3

THE IMPACT OF VARYING THE VALUE OF STATISTICAL LIFE AND DISCOUNT RATE ON AGGREGATE NET BENEFITS

(*n* = 106)

VSL	Discount Rate				
	1%	3%	5%	7%	9%
$1 million	538	414	329	267	218
$3 million	1,503	1,232	1,053	924	826
$5 million	2,468	2,050	1,776	1,581	1,434
$7 million	3,433	2,868	2,500	2,239	2,042
$9 million	4,398	3,686	3,223	2,896	2,650

SOURCE: Author's calculations.
NOTES: Net benefits are in billions of 1995 dollars. VSL is in millions of 1994 dollars.

For all the sensitivity analyses discussed, the VSL varies from $1 million to $9 million and the discount rate varies from 1 percent to 9 percent. Baseline information is presented in table 3, which illustrates the impact of varying the discount rate and the value of a statistical life on the aggregate net benefits of major final regulations passed between 1981 and mid-1996.[132] The number in each cell of the table indicates the aggregate net benefits of final regulations in billions of dollars, corresponding to a specific VSL and discount rate. Aggregate net benefits are $1.8 trillion in the base case, corresponding to a discount rate of 5 percent and a VSL of $5 million. This table shows that aggregate net benefits of final regulations are positive and significant for the entire range of assumptions.

Table 4 shows the fraction of regulations that pass a cost-benefit test based on the quantifiable benefits and costs. The table reveals that, in the base case, 43 percent of the 106 regulations pass a cost-benefit test.[133] The fraction of regulations that pass such a test ranges between 35 and 45 percent, depending on the scenario. As the VSL increases and the discount rate decreases, more regulations pass a cost-benefit test.

TABLE 4

THE IMPACT OF VARYING THE VALUE OF STATISTICAL LIFE AND
DISCOUNT RATE ON REGULATIONS PASSING A COST-BENEFIT TEST
(*n* = 106)

VSL	Discount Rate				
	1%	3%	5%	7%	9%
$1 million	38%	38%	37%	36%	35%
$3 million	41%	41%	41%	40%	40%
$5 million	43%	43%	43%	42%	42%
$7 million	43%	43%	43%	42%	42%
$9 million	45%	45%	43%	42%	42%

SOURCE: Author's calculations.
NOTES: VSL is in millions of 1994 dollars. Each estimate represents the percentage of
regulations that pass a cost-benefit test.

Benefits

There are two general critiques of my work on benefits. First, many
rules that are likely to have positive benefits are assigned zero benefits. Second, the value of a statistical life used in the study is too low.

The Zero Benefits Critique. Parker finds it problematic that I
assign a zero benefit to some regulations for which the agency narrates some benefits but does not quantify any.[134] In that part of the
study, I was interested in quantifying and monetizing those benefits and costs that could reasonably be quantified and monetized.

Yet, Parker makes a "startling discovery" that 41 of the 136 regulations in the database are assigned a zero benefit.[135] Since I note in
the regulatory scorecard that agencies monetized benefits[136] for only
26 percent of all rules between 1981 and 1996, Parker should not be
surprised to find that some regulations are assigned zero benefits.[137]

As noted in the study, I went to some lengths to monetize
quantities, *particularly on the benefit side*, where an agency had not

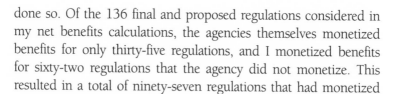

done so. Of the 136 final and proposed regulations considered in my net benefits calculations, the agencies themselves monetized benefits for only thirty-five regulations, and I monetized benefits for sixty-two regulations that the agency did not monetize. This resulted in a total of ninety-seven regulations that had monetized benefits in my database.138

Parker claims that the study assigns a zero value to any benefit not quantified and monetized by the agency, *with a few exceptions*.139 However, monetizing benefits for sixty-two regulations that the agency did not monetize is not indicative of "a few exceptions." In fact, I monetized benefits that the agency did not monetize for approximately half of all regulations. Parker, on the other hand, does not offer a proposal for monetizing unquantified benefits. Moreover, I did not simply "disregard whole categories of benefits," as Parker suggests, but considered them in four ways. First, as noted earlier, in the regulatory scorecard, I indicated the number of rules for which the RIAs did not monetize benefits.140 Second, I did sensitivity analyses on the benefit and cost numbers to determine the extent to which they affected the basic results.141 Third, this study gave rise to subsequent work that focused on this issue in more detail.142 Finally, I made it evident that part of the study would focus on quantifiable benefits and costs.143

A key objection is that I assign a zero benefit to some regulations for which the agency narrates some benefits but does not quantify any. This is true, but I never claimed otherwise. Moreover, there was no simple alternative to filling gaps in an agency's analysis. It might be useful to do another study focusing on narrated benefits and costs, but that was not the focus of my study. In addition, it is relatively easy for an agency to narrate benefits or costs; it is another matter to quantify them.144

I assign zero benefits to these regulations for lack of a better assumption. Some would argue that zero is a lower bound and can lead to misleading results. I would argue that this is a matter of interpretation. For example, if a regulation had some quantified costs, and benefits were assigned a zero value, then quantifiable net benefits would be negative, and the regulation would not pass a cost-benefit test based on quantifiable net benefits. But the regulation could still pass a more broadly defined cost-benefit test if nonquantifiable benefits were included in the final decision.[145]

Homeland security regulations provide a good example. So far, it has been very difficult to quantify the benefits of those regulations. At the same time, we would argue that it is useful to put pressure on the agency to try to quantify the benefits of those regulations to the extent feasible to avoid wasteful social expenditures.

In short, I think it is not unreasonable to assign a zero dollar value to unquantified benefits and cost categories for three reasons. First, it would provide regulatory agencies with an incentive to provide more information on quantifiable benefits and costs. Second, any other assumption seems totally arbitrary since I have no information on the actual nonquantified benefits and costs.[146] Third, the measure of *quantifiable* net benefits should be used in conjunction with nonquantifiable benefits and costs to reach a decision. Exactly how is a matter of some debate.[147]

Some of the rules with zero benefits are so-called process regulations, such as a regulation that would increase the costs of getting permits to operate a plant.[148] I consider later the impact of excluding the regulations assigned zero benefits.

Value of Life Is Too Low. My study used a VSL of $3 million to $7 million, with a most likely value of $5 million.[149] I based this choice of estimates on a review of the literature and a discussion with economic experts within and outside the government.[150]

Parker suggests that my best estimate and range for the VSL are not appropriate.[151] In fact, several studies and guidance documents would support my general range. The OMB's guidelines during the Clinton administration and draft guidelines during the current Bush administration are instructive.[152] A meta-analysis of several studies by Viscusi and Aldy places the median value at $7 million (in year 2000 dollars) for a worker in the United States.[153] However, Parker adjusts Hahn's values in ways that would increase the value of life by a factor of 3.5–5.5.[154] These ways include a number of adjustments for growth in real income and involuntary risks.[155] Parker does not

TABLE 5

THE IMPACT OF EXCLUDING REGULATIONS WITH ZERO BENEFITS
ON REGULATIONS PASSING A COST-BENEFIT TEST
(n = 74)

VSL	Discount Rate				
	1%	3%	5%	7%	9%
$1 million	51%	51%	50%	49%	47%
$3 million	55%	55%	55%	54%	54%
$5 million	59%	59%	59%	58%	58%
$7 million	59%	59%	59%	58%	58%
$9 million	62%	62%	59%	58%	58%

SOURCE: Author's calculations.
NOTES: VSL is in millions of 1994 dollars. Each estimate represents the percentage of
regulations that pass a cost-benefit test.

explain how he derives many of his estimates, including the adjustments for inflation, income growth, and income elasticity of risk.
Moreover, Parker concedes that his estimates are speculative.[156]

Such adjustments were reviewed by the EPA's Science Advisory
Board (SAB) and generally not supported due to uncertainties
regarding the adjustments.[157] Therefore, Parker's adjustments are
questionable at best. In other words, Parker claims that my estimates are inappropriate, even though they are based on many studies, and offers his own, which he admits are speculative.

In short, my range and estimate for the VSL were reasonable.
I next consider some sensitivities to address the concerns of those
who disagree with this assessment.

Analytical Response to Critique of Benefits. This section provides
some quantitative information on the various critiques related to
benefits. Table 5 illustrates the impact of deleting regulations with
zero monetized benefits from the data set. When final rules with zero
benefits are excluded, 59 percent of the remaining seventy-four regulations pass a cost-benefit test in the base case. The percentage of

TABLE 6

THE INCREMENTAL IMPACT OF ADDING NONSTANDARD BENEFITS ON REGULATIONS PASSING A COST-BENEFIT TEST

(*n* = 106)

VSL	Discount Rate				
	1%	3%	5%	7%	9%
$1 million	2%	2%	2%	2%	3%
$3 million	2%	2%	2%	2%	2%
$5 million	2%	2%	2%	2%	2%
$7 million	2%	2%	2%	2%	2%
$9 million	2%	2%	2%	2%	2%

SOURCE: Author's calculations.
NOTES: VSL is in millions of 1994 dollars. Each estimate represents the increase in percentage of regulations that pass a cost-benefit test.

TABLE 7

THE INCREASE IN PERCENTAGE OF REGULATIONS PASSING A COST-BENEFIT TEST WITH NONSTANDARD BENEFITS

(excluding regulations with zero benefits)

VSL	Discount Rate				
	1%	3%	5%	7%	9%
$1 million	1%	1%	1%	1%	3%
$3 million	1%	1%	1%	1%	1%
$5 million	1%	1%	1%	1%	1%
$7 million	1%	1%	1%	1%	1%
$9 million	1%	1%	1%	1%	1%

SOURCE: Author's calculations.
NOTES: VSL is in millions of 1994 dollars. Each estimate represents the increase in percentage of regulations that pass a cost-benefit test.

regulations that pass such a test varies from 47 percent when the VSL is very low and the discount rate is very high to 62 percent when the VSL is very high and the discount rate is very low. A significant percentage of regulations would fail a cost-benefit test under all assumptions even when rules with zero benefits are excluded.[158]

Parker also notes that I assign a zero value to "nonstandard" benefits, which the agency monetized.[159] Tables 6 and 7 illustrate that including "nonstandard" benefits in our calculation has very little effect on the percentage of rules that pass a cost-benefit test.[160] Table 6 shows that, when nonstandard benefits are included, only two rules that did not pass a cost-benefit test now pass a cost-benefit test in almost all the cases considered. Table 7 illustrates the same point about including nonstandard benefits for the case where zero benefit rules are excluded: The table reveals that only one rule that did not pass a cost-benefit test now passes a cost-benefit test in almost all cases.[161]

One of the problems that the critics correctly point out is that many benefits are missing from calculations of monetized benefits.[162] Hahn, Lutter, and Viscusi address this problem by restricting their sample to regulations where they estimate that mortality reductions accounted for at least 90 percent of total benefits, according to agency estimates.[163] Their results are summarized in table 8, in terms of net benefits and cost per statistical life saved. Several points are worth noting. First, aggregate net benefits for the regulations considered are positive, consistent with one of my earlier findings.[164] Second, just ten of twenty-four rules (42 percent) pass a cost-benefit test, again broadly consistent with my earlier findings. Third, net benefits of individual regulations span a wide range, from –$1.1 billion to $58.7 billion.

The other main critique of the benefits was that the value of a statistical life was too low. I consider here a range of $1 million to $9 million, as opposed to the $3 million to $7 million range in the original study. The change has a modest impact.[165] The net benefits of regulation remain positive for all scenarios. Moreover, the number of regulations passing a benefit-cost test approaches 50 percent in many of the best-case scenarios.[166]

TABLE 8
COSTS, BENEFITS, AND COSTS PER STATISTICAL LIFE SAVED OF
INDIVIDUAL REGULATIONS

Rule	Agency	Date
Toxicity characteristic	EPA	1990
Underground storage tanks: technical requirements	EPA	1988
Manufactured home construction and safety standards on wind standards	HUD	1994
Process safety management of highly hazardous chemicals	DOL	1992
Regulations restricting the sale and distribution of cigarettes and smokeless tobacco to protect children and adolescents	HHS	1996
Medicare and Medicaid programs: hospital conditions of participation, identification of potential organ, tissue, and eye donors and transplant hospitals' provision of transplant-related data	HHS	1998
Quality mammography standards	HHS	1997
Food labeling regulations	HHS	1993
Childproof lighters	CPSC	1993
Standard for occupational exposure to benzene	DOL	1987
Occupational exposure to methylene chloride	DOL	1997
Occupational exposure to 4,4' methylenedianiline	DOL	1992
Asbestos; manufacture, importation, processing, and distribution in commerce prohibitions (total)	EPA	1989
National primary and secondary water regulations, Phase II: MCLs for 38 contaminants (total, not incremental costs)	EPA	1991
Occupational exposure to asbestos	DOL	1994

Gross cost	Cost savings	Total costs	Monetized benefits	Net benefits	Total cost per statistical life saved
233	629	–397	0.17	397	–8,300
3,279	3,667	–388	3.9	392	–354
56	111	–55	8.1	63	–37
649	1,368	–719	1,197	1,916	–3.30
171	2,538	–2,368	56,330	58,698	–0.50
159	0	159	3,775	3,616	0.22
40	16	24	141	117	0.32
179	0	179	1,967	1,788	0.35
92	42	50	515	465	0.53
32	0	32	16	–16	7.13
103	0	103	125	23	8.46
12	0	12	2.5	–10	17.55
74	0	74	14	–61	19
1,096	0	1,096	156	–940	25
340	0	340	49	–291	27

(continued on next page)

(continued from previous page)

Rule	Agency	Date
Hazardous waste management system, wood preservatives (option D was selected as the final rule)	EPA	1990
Sewage sludge use and disposal regulations, 40 CFR part 503	EPA	1993
Land disposal restrictions for third scheduled waste	EPA	1990
Hazardous waste management system: final solvents and dioxins land disposal restrictions rule	EPA	1986
Occupational exposure to formaldehyde	DOL	1987
Prohibit the land disposal of the first third of scheduled wastes ("second sixth" proposal), alternative A	EPA	1988
Land disposal restrictions Phase II, universal treatment standards and treatment standards for organic toxicity, characteristic wastes, and newly listed wastes	EPA	1994
Drinking water regulations, synthetic organic chemicals, Phase V	EPA	1992
Solid waste disposal facility criteria, 40 CFR parts 257 and 258	EPA	1991
Totals	—	—

SOURCE: Adapted from Robert W. Hahn, Randall W. Lutter, and W. Kip Viscusi, *Do Federal Regulations Reduce Mortality?* (Washington, D.C.: AEI-Brookings Joint Center for Regulatory Studies, 2000).

Three key conclusions are to be drawn from this analysis. First, expanding the range for the VSL and discount rate has a minimal impact on the fraction of rules passing a cost-benefit test. Second, removing regulations with zero net benefits does not affect the conclusion that a significant number of regulations fail a cost-benefit test. And third, adding nonstandard, monetized benefits has only a small incremental impact on the results.

Gross cost	Cost savings	Total costs	Monetized benefits	Net benefits	Total cost per statistical life saved
14	0	14	1.0	−13	50
45	0	45	0.86	−44	185
515	1.2	514	10	−504	185
201	0	201	3.6	−197	197
82	0	82	0.75	−82	385.52
1,146	0	1,146	10	−1,135	399
223	79	144	0.56	−143	912
59	0	59	0.022	−59	9,550
186	9	176	0.017	−176	35,903
9,000	8,500	520	64,000	64,000	—

NOTE: All values are millions of 1995 dollars annually.

Costs

There are two general critiques of my work on costs. First, the study excludes some unquantified costs; second, the study excludes cost savings.[167]

Exclusion of Unquantified Costs. The study does exclude potentially important costs because it takes costs provided by the agencies as given. The agencies typically estimate direct costs, such as end-of-pipe costs. Examples could include the cost of a catalytic converter for a vehicle or the cost of putting a scrubber on a power plant. Such costs do not consider the lost profits, for example, that may be associated with a reduction in supply.[168] The agency analyses typically do not consider a number of other factors, such as possible increases in risk associated with regulations that reduce pollution.[169] In addition, the analyses typically do not consider economy-wide impact and the impact on management's time.[170]

The critics tend to miss an important implication related to the argument, that not all important costs are included. The argument is simple: If important costs are excluded, then it is virtually impossible to argue that there is a clear antiregulatory bias in the kinds of cost and cost-benefit analyses that have been considered here. Nonetheless, this is exactly what the critics tend to do.[171] The reality is that the bias in costs and benefits relative to the costs and benefits associated with implementation is difficult to discern.[172]

Exclusion of Cost Savings. Parker claims that I exclude cost savings from my analysis.[173] This claim is incorrect because I include cost savings in the analysis in several places.[174] The issue of cost savings is complicated. Sometimes the savings an agency identifies in its regulatory analysis are reasonable, but other times such cost savings may result in the "double counting" of benefits.[175]

A good illustration is energy savings associated with a particular technology. Suppose a consumer pays less for electricity by purchasing a more energy-efficient air conditioner. Then the dollar savings from the reduction in electricity use should not be added in a second time as cost savings, since it would already be included in the costs of operating the unit. Including the cost savings would result in double counting benefits. It is generally considered prudent to avoid double counting in cost-benefit analysis.[176]

IV

IN SUPPORT OF REGULATORY SCORECARDS AND THE ECONOMIC ANALYSIS OF REGULATION

This section identifies five key contributions that regulatory score-cards and economic analysis have made to our overall understanding of social policies and regulations. Moreover, I argue that this kind of economic analysis is not antiregulatory as many of the critics claim. Finally, I suggest that the critics have not offered a viable alternative to scorecards and economic analysis.

Scorecards and Economic Analysis Provide Useful Information on the Effectiveness of Regulatory Policies

A well-known result is that cost-effectiveness frequently varies over a wide range for regulations and other policy interventions, including health and the environment.[177] A variety of studies illustrate this result. Morrall's original table, which received significant attention from the critics, suggests that the cost per life saved varies over several orders of magnitude.[178] Despite the criticisms, that finding turns out to be fairly robust for federal regulations. Using some of the same RIAs he examined, I derive a similar result.[179] Morrall also has a similar finding in a recent paper, which builds on earlier work with Lutter.[180] Table 8, which is based on Hahn, Lutter, and Viscusi's work on mortality reductions from regulations, reveals that cost-effectiveness for the regulations they examined aimed primarily at saving lives ranges from less than zero to almost $36 billion per statistical life saved.[181] The analysis by Tengs, Graham, and others also supports the general finding that the cost-effectiveness of regulations and interventions, measured in cost per life-year saved, varies over several orders of magnitude.[182]

A large number of analyses in the environmental area examine the potential and actual cost savings of tradable emission permits

FIGURE 2

RANGES IN INCREMENTAL CONTROL COSTS FOR EXISTING AND
NEW-SOURCE STANDARDS IN VARIOUS INDUSTRIES

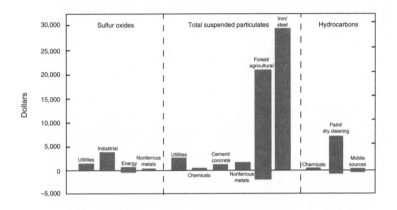

SOURCE: Adapted from figure 3-1 in Robert W. Crandall, *Controlling Industrial Pollution: The Economics and Politics of Clean Air* (Washington, D.C.: The Brookings Institution, 1983).

versus command-and-control regulation.[183] The estimate of these cost savings is premised on differences in the cost-effectiveness of pollution control among different sources of pollution.[184] Tradable permits and other economic approaches provide incentives for firms with relatively low pollution control costs to cut their emissions.[185]

An early example of this analysis is shown in figure 2.[186] The analysis, by Crandall, illustrates the wide range of pollution control costs for existing sources. The wide range of pollution control costs per unit of pollution suggests that significant savings may be accrued in achieving the same pollution goal by introducing economic incentives, such as tradable permits.

In the public health arena, there are also significant differences among the cost-effectiveness of different interventions, using different measures of effectiveness. Tengs et al. find that variations in cost-effectiveness exist between categories of life-saving interventions.[187] Interestingly, the public health literature also makes widespread use of "scorecards."[188]

A second important finding related to cost-effectiveness is that federal regulations aimed at reducing cancer are, on average, less cost-effective than regulations aimed at enhancing safety. This finding first came to light in 1986 in Morrall's "A Review of the Record."[189] Table 9 is an updated version of Morrall's original table and presents the cost-effectiveness of seventy-six regulatory actions promulgated by the federal government from 1967 to 2001. The results from this table confirm his original conclusions that wide differences in cost-effectiveness indicate that we can save lives more effectively.[190]

Several studies have shown how the cost-effectiveness of policy interventions varies across programs. For example, in a seminal study of Superfund, Professors Hamilton and Viscusi found that costs per cancer case averted are very high at most of the Superfund sites in their sample, with only 44 out of 145 sites having a marginal cost per cancer case averted of less than $100 million.[191]

Although cost-effectiveness estimates can illustrate the desirability of a regulation, in principle, a better measure of desirability is net social benefits.[192] Similar findings arise from comparing net benefits of different programs and regulations. My work suggests a wide range of net benefits across federal regulations. In addition, as noted already, a significant fraction of regulations are likely to fail a cost-benefit test based on quantifiable benefits and costs associated with the government's numbers.[193] The work by Hahn, Lutter, and Viscusi, summarized in table 8, also supports this view.

In a perceptive analysis of the costs and benefits of different environmental policies, Freeman concludes that some policies are economic winners and others are losers. Winners include removing lead from gas, controlling particulate matter in air pollution, reducing lead in drinking water, cleaning up hazardous waste sites with the lowest cost per cancer case avoided, and controlling chlorofluorocarbon emissions. These policies are similar in that they consider

TABLE 9

OPPORTUNITY COSTS PER STATISICAL LIFE SAVED (OCSLS)

Regulation	Year Issued	Agency	OCSLS (2002 $ millions)
Childproof Lighters	1993	CPSC	0.1
Respiratory Protection	1998	OSHA-H	0.1
Logging Operations	1994	OSHA-S	0.1
Electrical Safety	1990	OSHA-S	0.1
Steering Column Protection	1967	NHTSA	0.2
Unvented Space Heaters	1980	CPSC	0.2
Safety Standards for Scaffolds	1996	OSHA-S	0.2
Cabin Fire Protection	1985	FAA	0.3
Trihalomethanes	1979	EPA	0.3
Organ Procurement Regulations	1998	HHS	0.3
AED on Large Planes	2001	FAA	0.3
Mammography Sts.	1997	HHS	0.4
Food Labeling Regulations	1993	FDA	0.4
Stability and Control during Braking/Trucks	1995	NHTSA	0.4
Electrical Power Generation	1994	OSHA-S	0.4
Passive Restraints/Belts	1984	NHTSA	0.5
Fuel System Integrity	1975	NHTSA	0.5
Underground Construction	1983	OSHA-S	0.5
Head Impact Protection	1995	NHTSA	0.7
Alcohol and Drug Control	1985	FRA	0.9
Servicing Wheel Rims	1984	OSHA-S	0.9
Reflective Devices for Heavy Trucks	1999	NHTSA	0.9
Seat Cushion Flammability	1984	FAA	1.0
Side Impact and Autos	1990	NHTSA	1.1
Medical Devices	1996	FDA	1.1
Floor Emergency Lighting	1984	FAA	1.2
Crane Suspended Personnel Platform	1984	OSHA-S	1.5
Low-Altitude Windshear	1988	FAA	1.8
Electrical Equipment Sts./ Metal Mines	1970	MSHA	1.9
Trenching and Excavation	1989	OSHA-S	2.1

Regulation	Year Issued	Agency	OCSLS (2002 $ millions)
Traffic Alert and Collision Avoidance	1988	FAA	2.1
Children's Sleepware Flammability	1973	CPSC	2.2
Side Doors	1970	NHTSA	2.2
Concrete and Masonry Construction	1985	OSHA-S	2.4
Confined Spaces	1993	OSHA-S	2.5
Hazard Communication	1983	OSHA-S	3.1
Child Restraints	1999	NHTSA	3.3
Benzene/Fugitive Emissions	1984	EPA	3.7
Rear/Up/Shoulder Belts/Autos	1989	NHTSA	4.4
Asbestos	1972	OSHA-H	5.5
EDB Drinking Water Sts.	1991	EPA	6.0
NO$_x$ SIP Call	1998	EPA	6.0
Benzene/Revised: Coke By-Products	1988	EPA	6.4
Radionuclides/Uranium Mines	1984	EPA	6.9
Roadway Worker Protection	1997	FRA	7.1
Grain Dust	1988	OSHA-S	11
Electrical Equipment Sts./Coal Mines	1970	MSHA	13
Methylene Chloride	1997	OSHA-H	13
Arsenic/Glass Paint	1986	EPA	19
Benzene	1987	OSHA-H	22
Arsenic/Copper Smelter	1986	EPA	27
Uranium Mill Tailings/Inactive	1983	EPA	28
Hazardous Wastes Listing for Petroleum Sludge	1990	EPA	29
Acrylonitrile	1978	OSHA-H	31
Benzene/Revised: Transfer Operations	1990	EPA	35
4.4 methylenedianiline	1992	OSHA-H	36
Coke Ovens	1976	OSHA-H	51
Nat. Primary/Secondary Drinking Water Regulations Phase II	1991	EPA	50
Uranium Mill Tailings/Active	1983	EPA	53

(continued on next page)

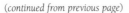

(continued from previous page)

Regulation	Year Issued	Agency	OCSLS (2002 $ millions)
Asbestos	1986	OSHA-H	66
Asbestos/Construction	1994	OSHA	71
Arsenic	1978	OSHA-H	77
Asbestos Ban	1989	EPA	78
Ethylene Oxide	1984	OSHA-H	80
Lockout/Tagout	1989	OSHA-S	98
Hazardous Waste Management/ Wood Products	1990	EPA	140
DES (Cattlefeed)	1979	FDA	170
Benzene/Revised: Waste Operations	1990	EPA	180
Sewage Sludge Disposal	1993	EPA	530
Land Disposal Restrictions	1990	EPA	530
Hazardous Waste: Solids Dioxin	1986	EPA	560
Prohibit Land Disposal	1988	EPA	1,100
Land Disposal Restrictions: Phase II	1994	EPA	2,600
Drinking Water: Phase II	1992	EPA	19,000
Formaldehyde	1987	OSHA-H	78,000
Solid Waste Disposal Facility Criteria	1991	EPA	100,000

SOURCE: Adapted from table 3 in John Morrall, "Saving Lives: A Review of the Record," *Journal of Risk and Uncertainty* 27 (2003): 221–37.

threats to human health, especially mortality, and the widespread exposure of people.[194]

Freeman's losers include mobile source air pollution control, most waterway discharge control, many regulations under the Federal Insecticide, Fungicide and Rodenticide Act, the Toxic Substances Control Act, the Safe Drinking Water Act, and Superfund, and policies aimed at controlling ground-level ozone.[195]

All the quantitative studies cited here use some form of scorecard, either implicitly or explicitly, to reach conclusions about the relative effectiveness of different policy interventions. They show that scorecards using cost-effectiveness and net benefits measures have yielded important insights into the effectiveness of policy.

Scorecards and Economic Analysis Set the Stage for Smarter Regulation

Perhaps less appreciated by the critics is that scorecards and related economic analysis have been helpful in initiating smarter regulatory policies. By "smarter" regulation, I refer to policies that allow one to achieve a particular social objective at a lower overall social cost.[196]

One well-known example is the application of market-based approaches for achieving environmental objectives.[197] Table 10, modified from table 4 in Tietenberg, highlights estimated potential cost savings in moving from a command-and-control regulatory regime to a market-based approach, such as one relying on emissions trading.[198] These savings accrue because of the differences in estimated cost-effectiveness of different control strategies. Having demonstrated these potential cost savings, researchers began to have an impact on legislators and regulators, who eventually implemented some of these ideas.[199]

Another example is the identification of policies that could inadvertently increase health risks when they are aimed at reducing risks.[200] Sunstein identifies a number of such policies in his book, including fuel economy standards designed to reduce environmental risks but that may make automobiles less safe, banning the manufacture and use of asbestos that may lead companies to use more dangerous substitutes, and efforts to remove asbestos from schools that may cause serious risks to workers.[201] When researchers and government policy analysts quantify such risk-risk tradeoffs with scorecards,[202] they provide an incentive for regulatory agencies to examine these issues more closely and possibly avoid regulations where risk-risk tradeoffs are not acceptable.[203]

Another set of issues closely related to risk-risk comparisons are health-wealth tradeoffs. It has been widely observed that greater wealth is associated with greater health and longer lives. As incomes

TABLE 10
POTENTIAL COST SAVINGS FROM MARKET-BASED
POLLUTION CONTROL

Study and Year	Pollutants	Ratio of Command-and-Control Cost to Least Cost
Atkinson and Lewis (1974)	Particulates	6
Roach et al. (1981)	Sulfur dioxide	4
Hahn and Noll (1982)	Sulfates	1
Krupnick (1983)	Nitrogen dioxide	6
Seskin, Anderson, and Reid (1983)	Nitrogen dioxide	14
McGartland (1984)	Particulates	4
Spofford (1984)	Sulfur dioxide	2
Harrison (1983)	Airport noise	2
Maloney and Yandle (1984)	Hydrocarbons	4
Palmer, Mooz, Quinn, and Wolf (1980)	Chlorofluorocarbon emissions, nonaerosol applications	2

SOURCE: Adapted from table 4 in Thomas H. Tietenberg, *Emissions Trading: An Exercise in Reforming Pollution Policy* (Washington, D.C.: Resources for the Future, 1985). NOTES: Numbers are rounded to the nearest whole number. A cost ratio equal to 1 implies that the command-and-control allocation is cost effective, and therefore the potential cost savings are zero. A ratio greater than 1 implies cost savings.

increase, people spend more money on health care and products that reduce risk, such as safer cars. As incomes decrease, people spend less on risk reduction.[204] A regulation that is very cost ineffective reduces income and could thus increase the total risk to the community.[205] Hahn, Lutter, and Viscusi studied twenty-four regulations designed to save lives and found that only about half were likely to reduce net mortality.[206] By quantifying such health-wealth tradeoffs, this research provides an incentive for regulatory agencies to examine these issues more closely and consider avoiding such regulations. In addition, scholars such as Keeney,[207] Viscusi,[208]

Lutter,[209] and others have examined the link at the margin between income and health. These studies attempt to find the amount of regulatory expenditure required to induce one fatality. The most recent study by Lutter et al. found that every $15 million in regulatory expenditures induces one fatality.[210]

A comparison of regulations based on net benefits or cost-effectiveness can also be used to identify regulations or regulatory opportunities that yield a higher social return for a given expenditure, such as saving more lives for a given expenditure.[211] In a paper responding to the critics, Morrall identifies four such regulatory opportunities: reducing the intake of trans fatty acids by requiring labeling, requiring bar codes for drugs and biologic products, promoting automatic defibrillators in the workplace, and promoting foods containing omega-3 fatty acids.[212]

Scorecards Help with the Development of New Techniques to Assess the Quality of Regulatory Analysis and Oversight

One of the uses of scorecards not fully appreciated by the critics is to assess the extent to which agencies consider certain key variables in their RIAs. Scorecards provide a systematic way of addressing these issues.[213]

For example, Hahn et al. find a number of revealing quantitative and qualitative facts concerning a sample of forty-eight RIAs from the Clinton administration. While overall, the RIAs nearly always (96 percent) give at least a narrative description of benefits, only about 70 percent quantified those benefits and a little less than half monetized those benefits. But the RIAs examined in the study failed to provide both a best estimate and a range of quantified or monetized benefits for over 80 percent of the rules.[214] Only about one half of the rules provided an estimate of either net benefits or cost-effectiveness. Only one quarter of the rules in the sample quantified information on the costs and benefits of alternatives to the regulation. This scorecard approach reveals that it is possible to score both qualitative and quantitative information.[215]

Scorecards that attempt to provide insight into the quality of regulatory analysis have some obvious limitations. For example, they do not tell us much about the quality of the underlying science or whether the agency estimates are accurate.[216] Nor do scorecards tell us how economic analysis influenced the final decision. However, when considered in conjunction with case studies of particular regulations or groups of regulations, they can provide an informative picture of how well regulatory analysis is performed.[217]

Scorecards can also be used to study reports on the costs and benefits of regulation. Recently, Hahn and Muething examined the annual OMB reports to Congress on the costs and benefits of federal regulation. By scoring the first five OMB reports, they found some interesting trends. First, a majority of RIAs for new rules examined in the last four reports quantify some measure of costs and benefits. Second, the last four reports reveal that benefits are monetized less frequently than costs. Third, a small number of RIAs quantify neither costs nor benefits.[218]

Analysis of the OMB reports can also provide insights into the quality of OMB oversight. The OMB takes the agency's analyses of the expected economic impacts of regulations as given, monetizes benefits where it can, and does not revisit the assumptions or numbers in the agency's analyses. Whatever an agency's RIA says is gospel for the purposes of the OMB's analysis.[219] Using the agency's numbers, the OMB reports on the aggregate net benefits of regulation, but it does not report on the number of regulations that are likely to pass a cost-benefit test by category. I believe information on the number of regulations that pass a cost-benefit test is potentially useful to decision makers. If a large fraction of regulations passed a cost-benefit test in particular categories, some have argued that there might be less need for oversight.[220]

I used a scorecard to examine the number of regulations that passed a cost-benefit test using OMB's assumptions. I then compared that with the number that passed using my assumptions from a prior study. I considered twenty-one regulations that overlap with an analysis that I authored. Table 11 compares the results of my analysis with the OMB's.

TABLE 11

COST-BENEFIT COMPARISON FOR REGULATIONS THAT OVERLAP

Regulation	Pass Cost-Benefit Test?	
	OMB[a]	Hahn
Department of Labor		
Confined Spaces	1[b]	1
Occupational Exposure to Asbestos	0	0
Department of Transportation		
Vessel Response Plans	0	0
Double-Hull Standards	0	0
Stability Control of Medium and Heavy Vehicles during Braking	1	1
Environmental Protection Agency		
Oil and Gas Extraction	1	0
Acid Rain Permits	1	1
Vehicle Inspection and Maintenance	1	1
Evaporative Emissions from Light-Duty Vehicles	1	1
Phase II Land Disposal	0	0
Phase-out of Ozone-Depleting Chemicals	1	1
Reformulated Gasoline	0	0
Acid Rain NO_x Title IV	1	1
Hazardous Organic NESHAP	1	1
Refueling Emissions from Light-Duty Vehicles	1	1
Non-Road Compression Ignition Engines	1	1
Deposit Control Gasoline	1	1
Onboard Diagnostics	1	0
Health and Human Services		
Food Labeling (combined analysis of 23 individual rules)	1	1
Housing and Urban Development		
Manufactured Housing Wind Standards	1	1
Department of Agriculture		
Nutrition Labeling of Meat	1	1
Total Number Passed	16	14
Percentage	76%	67%

SOURCES: OMB (2003), Hahn (2000). Adapted from Robert W. Hahn and Rohit Malik, "Is Regulation Good for You?" *Harvard Journal of Law and Public Policy* 27, no. 3 (2004): 893–916.
a. The OMB cost and benefit estimates were calculated by finding the midpoint estimate of the reported cost and benefit ranges in the OMB 2003 Report. 1=Yes, 0= No.
b. A regulation is ruled to have passed a cost-benefit test if its estimated benefits exceed its estimated costs.

While the two methods for assessing benefits and costs differ in terms of valuing both benefits and costs, both take the agency analyses as the basic point of departure. The table reveals that the OMB finds that sixteen of twenty-one regulations pass a cost-benefit test and I find that fourteen of twenty-one regulations pass a cost-benefit test. For the two regulations on which we differ, we have similar estimates of benefits and costs for one regulation, Oil and Gas Extraction. It just barely fails using my estimates. The discrepancy between the numbers on the other regulation, Onboard Diagnostics, results from different valuations of the benefits resulting from preventing certain pollution emissions. Thus, two somewhat different methodologies arrive at similar findings about which regulations are likely to pass a cost-benefit test. This scorecard leads me to the conclusion that the OMB numbers are plausible, given the methodology that the agency employed.

This discussion reveals that scorecards related to assessing the costs and benefits of regulations can do a lot more than Parker suggests. They are quite versatile instruments that have offered important insights.

Scorecards Help Make the Regulatory Process More Transparent and Hold Regulators More Accountable

A key goal of many scholars of regulation, including the critics, is to make the regulatory process more transparent.[221] In my early research on RIAs, I discovered some very simple problems with the presentation of information. For example, the executive summaries of RIAs frequently did not offer a best estimate of cost and benefits or describe those benefits.[222]

To address this problem, I helped develop a scorecard.[223] This scorecard summarizes key aspects of the regulation, such as the agency's estimates for both quantitative and qualitative costs and benefits, and promotes accountability by allowing the OMB and others to evaluate how well agencies report information. More recently, the Office of Information and Regulatory

Affairs (OIRA) adopted a scorecard that would serve a similar function.[224]

In addition to helping with regulatory transparency, scorecards can contribute to the development of institutions that hold regulators more accountable. One such institution is a regulatory budget. The idea behind a regulatory budget is to limit the costs a regulatory agency can impose on consumers and business through regulation.[225] The hope is that, by limiting such costs, regulators have a greater incentive to select regulations with a higher social payoff and limit regulations that are not very cost-effective. The key point for this discussion is that research on the cost of regulation, particularly for groups of regulations, could provide insights into the design of a regulatory budget or the design of an experiment to assess how well a regulatory budget would work in practice.[226]

Eric Posner suggested extending the idea of a regulatory budget to include benefits.[227] He suggests setting up "net benefit accounts" for agencies and describes how they would work. The idea is to give agencies a regulatory budget defined in terms of net benefits. If an agency passes a regulation that would increase net benefits, its regulatory budget would increase; if a regulation decreased net benefits, then its regulatory budget would decrease. The agencies would have an incentive to implement regulations with net benefits to increase the potential scope for regulatory activity. As with the earlier regulatory budget that focused on costs, the key point for this discussion is that research and scorecards on the net benefits of regulation could help in the design of net benefit accounts.

Scorecards Help with the Development of New Research Insights

Thus far, the critics have tended to focus their criticism on a few particular studies, most notably Morrall's early seminal work and subsequent work by Professors Tengs and Graham and myself. This critical approach fails to recognize how knowledge grows.

Research frequently has roots in earlier research. Work on the costs and benefits of federal regulation is no exception.

Over a decade ago, we began with some preliminary estimates of the costs and benefits of regulation, and scholars continue to refine those estimates in different ways.[228] A similar result has occurred with the cost-effectiveness of regulations. The work by Tengs et al. and the early work by Morrall represent important contributions to this debate. But perhaps they are more properly viewed as early contributions to an important subject rather than the final declaration. The same is true of my work that uses RIAs.

Fifteen years ago, for example, the issue of comparing projected costs and benefits with estimates after the fact (the ex-ante vs. ex-post issue) was not widely considered to be an important issue. Today, scholars and practitioners recognize that it could be an important issue.[229] In exploring this new research area, they can build on the large body of literature that relied on developing net benefit estimates using ex-ante estimates.[230]

Another example where scholars have built on knowledge, specifically related to Morrall's early work, is in trying to measure the effectiveness of the regulatory process.[231] The degree to which regulatory oversight makes an important difference is still hotly debated.

Scorecards Are Not Antiregulatory

Nothing is intrinsically antiregulatory about the scorecards that the critics decry. In the case of the work by Morrall and by Tengs and Graham, one interpretation is that this research could help highlight policy interventions that have not been attractive.[232] Another equally plausible interpretation is that such research helps highlight ways in which society can derive a better return on its regulatory investment.[233] Similarly, work on the net benefits of regulations may be used to reform or eliminate regulations. It can also be used to point out areas where more regulation might be needed. There is some evidence, for example, that more regulation is needed to address climate change issues, control fine particles in the air, and reduce indoor air pollution.[234] At the same time, we have probably over-regulated in other areas, such as controlling ground-level ozone.[235]

In short, the tools of economic analysis, and scorecards in particular, are not inherently antiregulatory or proregulatory.[236] The tools, if used judiciously, can help to strike an appropriate balance.[237]

What Is the Alternative?

Some critics claim that cost-benefit analysis is an "atomistic" or "reductionist" approach.[238] They argue that breaking a problem into its components, using cost-benefit analysis as typically applied, can result in the loss of important information[239] and answers that defy common sense.[240]

Heinzerling and Ackerman propose, as an alternative, using a "holistic" approach for analyzing costs and benefits, where costs as a whole and benefits as a whole are considered together but are not forced to be expressed in the same units.[241]

Heinzerling and Ackerman's critique of cost-benefit analysis as an analytical tool falls short on several counts. First, they do not acknowledge many advantages offered by cost-benefit analysis.[242] For example, cost-benefit analysis attempts to aggregate incremental benefits and costs to develop a measure, albeit imperfect, of the overall "net benefits" of a regulatory decision.[243] When done judiciously, cost-benefit analysis also considers whether other alternatives can result in higher levels of net benefits. In addition, when data are available, such analysis can provide assessments of economic impacts on particular subgroups within a population, thus assessing distributional or equity issues. It therefore provides a useful device for helping to reach an informed judgment about the relative merits of a policy.

Second, the fact that cost-benefit analysis can defy common sense is not necessarily a problem. Indeed, in many cases, it is a strength.[244] Take the example of arsenic. The EPA's analysis of this issue suggested that regulation of arsenic in drinking water to the most stringent of the contemplated standards would not pass a cost-benefit test.[245] Or, stated another way, the cost per statistical life saved under the most stringent arsenic standard appeared to be substantially higher than the benefits as measured by most plausible measures of willingness to pay.[246] Such information is useful for a decision maker, even if he decides to regulate arsenic to that stringent standard.

Third, contrary to what Heinzerling and Ackerman say, cost-benefit analysis does not require that costs and benefits be expressed in the same units or that agencies monetize benefits that may not be quantifiable.[247] Guidelines for cost-benefit analysis typically encourage analysts to monetize costs and benefits to the maximum extent reasonable. That does not mean, however, that other forms of analysis, such as cost-effectiveness analysis or risk-risk analysis, should not be considered.[248] They should be considered along with cost-benefit analysis.

Fourth, Heinzerling and Ackerman's alternative to weighing costs and benefits, a "holistic" approach, appears to require an implicit acceptance of a cost-benefit framework. Indeed, Ackerman and Heinzerling suggest that the two approaches would yield the same answer with full information.[249] If the two approaches yield the same answer with full information, it suggests that the authors would embrace the analytical framework. But, with partial information, the situation most relevant for real world problems, the only conceptual changes are the inclusion of uncertainty and accounting for diverse effects without quantifying them. That means one should be careful to reflect those uncertainties and account for qualitative factors in the underlying analysis.[250] It does not generally imply that the analysis, itself, should not be done. A decision maker can often benefit from having estimates of the distribution of monetary benefits and costs, along with other relevant information.

Fifth, Heinzerling and Ackerman never satisfactorily explain why some benefits are intrinsically "priceless," other than to suggest that they are not traded in markets.[251] The fact that it may be difficult to quantify or monetize certain incremental benefits, such as reducing mercury emissions, does not make them priceless. It merely means that the value people place on them is uncertain.

Sixth, the holistic approach does not provide guidance on *how much* to regulate. It does not, for example, help in setting the standard for particulate matter. The authors would appear to concede as much, stating that a "holistic assessment leads to an either-or-choice: to buy or not to buy."[252] But even here, the holistic approach falls short. The problem is that Heinzerling and Ackerman do not offer an approach to weigh things that are "priceless." If some things are "priceless," making a buy or not-buy choice is extremely difficult. Should "priceless" values trump all other benefits? Does one value a life today more than one tomorrow? How does one account for the risk-risk tradeoffs between the present and future? Heinzerling and Ackerman fail to answer these difficult but critical questions.

On the question of how much to buy, the authors offer three additional principles: follow moral imperatives rather than cost comparisons, adopt a precautionary approach, and promote fairness.[253] The authors endorse a holistic approach for weighing costs and benefits in making policy, but then they add other principles that should be factored into a decision.

This leads to a natural question. If one is indeed taking a holistic approach to costs and benefits, why are additional principles needed to guide decision making? In setting up these principles for decision making, the authors would seem to suggest that their holistic approach may not be a sufficient basis for reaching a decision. But, if their holistic approach is not sufficient, then their approach is by definition not holistic.

Even if one accepts these principles, they provide no clear basis for making decisions. Balancing these potentially competing principles means a very wide range of decisions could be justified in practice.[254] Following moral imperatives may or may not be consistent with a precautionary "no-risk" principle depending on how these principles are applied. Furthermore, there is no guarantee that following a precautionary approach or moral imperatives would necessarily be consistent with a holistic approach or fairness concerns in determining policy. Consider a stylized example. A holistic approach to analyzing costs and benefits of climate change could imply a $20 tax per ton of carbon emitted. A precautionary approach could involve a $100 tax per ton, or paralyze policy-making due to a desire to take precautions against both the risks of carbon and the risks of the carbon tax itself.255 Ackerman and Heinzerling neglect these pitfalls of the precautionary principle. Following a moral imperative, assuming we know which one to follow, might yield a $200 tax per ton or may not yield a clear policy.256 Fairness concerns could require subsidizing some groups that have to pay the tax. What is a poor policymaker to do?257

Finally, Heinzerling and Ackerman anticipate objections to their "alternative" by pointing out that many important decisions are made on the basis of rights and principles, not costs and benefits, and that major resource allocation decisions are often made without considering costs.258 The fact that many of government's decisions are made without regard to costs does not mean that cost-benefit analysis is not valuable for decision making.259 Indeed, this is another reason for applying the construct more broadly in areas ranging from homeland security to privacy.260

Another suggested alternative from the legal critic camp is to analyze regulation on a case-by-case basis.261 By and large, I think economists would be supportive of this approach. If the government is making a decision about a particular regulation, it makes sense to weigh the benefits and costs of that regulation. But what if the government or researchers are trying to assess the effectiveness of a program like Superfund?262 In such cases, studying regulations only on a case-by-case basis would not suffice. In some cases, there is no realistic alternative to measuring the impact of multiple regulations or statutes when the aim is to assess the effectiveness of a program.

In the words of one Nobel laureate economist, George Stigler, "[I]t takes a theory to beat a theory."263 The critics have failed to offer such a "theory." Until they do, we should continue with the current approach to analyzing social regulation, where cost-benefit analysis is supposed to play an important role, and remain open to changes in this analysis when they would furnish new insights.264

V

WHERE THE CRITICS AND I MAY CONVERGE

The critics and I agree on a number of points regarding the review of regulations. Here, I outline seven broad areas of potential agreement. I also note some areas where the critics and I might disagree on the details, even if we agree on the general theme.

Need to Weigh the Benefits against the Costs of Regulation

Some of the critics and I generally agree on the need to weigh benefits and costs of regulations.[265] But the agreement may stop there. Some of the critics believe that formal analysis is largely a waste of time.[266] They would rather have the administrator of a regulatory agency or Congress define a regulatory agenda without reference to formal analysis.[267]

As an economist, I believe that economic analysis is a very important input into decision making. As an economist schooled in political theory, I am also concerned about what will happen in the absence of some requirement to formally weigh costs and benefits and quantify them to the extent feasible. I fear that regulatory agencies and other mission-oriented agencies will be more inclined to pursue their narrow social agendas with less concern for either cost or effectiveness.[268] In short, I think they would be held less accountable because of difficulties in obtaining relevant information on costs and benefits.

Need to Balance Quantitative and Qualitative Information in Decision Making

Most people would agree that it is important to consider both quantitative and qualitative information on costs and benefits. As noted earlier, both the critics and I share that concern.[269]

Still, as several economists have argued, I think it is very important to quantify costs and benefits to the extent reasonable, especially in situations involving government regulation.[270] I believe the public has a right to know what it is getting when government mandates regulations. At the same time, qualitative factors should not be pushed into the background when there is some reason to think that they are important.

Note that, if some costs and all benefits are left out of the calculation, the direction of bias in the net benefits estimate is unclear. That is, the estimate could be high or low relative to some objective estimate of net benefits. This conclusion follows because we do not know how the unquantified costs and the unquantified benefits compare without further information.[271]

The challenge is how best to allow for adequate consideration of qualitative factors, and I suspect here is where the critics and I differ.[272] I would prefer that the regulator charged with making the decision on major regulations explain the basis for that decision, especially when quantitative estimation suggests that expected benefits fall significantly short of expected costs.[273] Like Justice Breyer, I believe agencies frequently suffer from tunnel vision,[274] and this constraint may help broaden that vision beyond the immediate mandate of the agency.

Need to Provide a Better Treatment of Uncertainty

Several scholars have made the point that there is a need to take better account of uncertainties. In general, some of the critics and I certainly agree here.[275] The treatment of uncertainty is an important issue.[276] It could, for example, lead to the conclusion that the estimates underlying regulation are more uncertain than initially thought.

At the same time, there is a legitimate question about how much uncertainty one should consider in doing analysis. This is a difficult issue and will depend on the problem being addressed and resource constraints.

Regulatory agencies have not adequately identified uncertainties in their analyses. For example, Hahn et al. found that of forty-eight RIAs published from April 1996 to July 1999, only 13 percent presented both a best estimate and a range of costs, and only 17 percent presented both a best estimate and a range of quantitative benefits.[277] Moreover, the existence of a range of estimates alone is a very superficial measure of the quality of the treatment of uncertainty. The ranges typically have ad hoc endpoints unrelated to probability distributions and so may not represent uncertainty better than no range at all.

Getting the agencies to do a better job of addressing uncertainty may not be easy. It has been tried in the past, apparently without much success. Earlier the OMB economic guidelines encouraged the agencies to consider uncertainty in their risk, benefit, and cost estimates and described methods to account for uncertainty.[278] The OMB recently provided guidance for economic analysis in which it suggests that agencies consider uncertainties.[279] It remains to be seen whether the agencies will actually follow this guidance.

Need to Consider Distributional Issues

The critics like to point out possible redistributional aspects of policies that could be important. They make a cogent appeal for considering distributional issues in regulatory policy.[280] While I agree with the importance of addressing distributional concerns, it is typically quite difficult to do properly, given data limitations. If the critics think that we should do more, then they should consider whether the additional expenditure is worth it. I would prefer to see resources first devoted to improving the quality of basic cost-benefit analysis done by regulatory agencies before significant resources are devoted to distributional issues. At the same time, I think it would be a good idea for government to fund research on ways to address distributional issues that would be helpful and cost effective.

Need to Do More Retrospective Analyses

Several scholars, including the critics, have pointed out problems with using ex-ante estimates of costs and benefits.[281] I agree, but doing retrospective analyses is costly. And the government often has little incentive to fund such analyses. Why would Congress or regulatory agencies want findings that suggest the decisions that they made turned out to be bad ones?[282] Nonetheless, I would support funding more research in this area and encouraging government to do more of its own work on this subject.

Need for Greater Regulatory Transparency

Critics lament the lack of transparency in the regulatory process, and so do I. They tend to be less pleased with transparency in regulatory oversight, and I tend to be less pleased with transparency in agency decision making.[283]

While I think transparency could and should be improved, it is important to recognize that both the regulatory agencies and the OMB have made significant strides in promoting transparency in recent years. The advent of the Web, government use of the Web, and widespread access to the Web mean that it is substantially easier to obtain information on government regulation than it was a decade ago. Many RIAs are now posted on the Web, whereas this was not true a decade ago when I started my research project.[284]

Need for New Institutional Approaches That Improve Regulation

The critics and I generally agree that regulation could be improved and some institutional changes are needed. But we frequently part company on the nature of appropriate solutions, as well as the nature of the problem. I think there are some serious defects in the regulatory process and regulatory policies.[285] Many of the regulatory critics would disagree.[286]

I believe some significant institutional changes are needed. For example, I would like to see Congress set up an office or agency outside of the executive branch to assess regulations both on a case-by-case basis and in the aggregate.[287]

Interestingly, Parker suggests something similar. He would like an external "ombudsman," such as Sunstein, with the credibility, independence, and detachment needed to do the job effectively.[288]

Justice Breyer suggests designing a more depoliticized regulatory process that draws on a centralized, administrative group with expertise in a number of disciplines. Such a group would develop a system for addressing risk-regulation, determining how to better allocate resource to reduce risks, and consisting of people familiar with science, risk analysis, economics, and administration.[289] I think that such a group could improve regulatory decision making, and the critics would probably agree.

The critics would also probably agree that the OMB should continue promoting efficient regulations by drafting "prompt letters" to agencies.[290] These letters are designed to prompt agencies to act in cases in which the benefits of action seem to outweigh the costs. Inspired by cost-benefit analysis, OIRA has asked OSHA to consider requiring that automatic defibrillators be placed in workplaces, has urged the FDA to issue a final rule requiring disclosure of the level of trans fatty acids in foods, and has asked the Department of Transportation to take steps to improve automobile safety by establishing a high-speed frontal offset crash test.[291] The critics would probably agree that such efforts result in improved regulation.[292]

I would also like to see greater experimentation with approaches that place some kind of budget constraint on regulatory agencies. This could take the form of a regulatory budget[293] or perhaps, Posner's suggestion of net benefit accounts.[294] I am fairly certain that the critics would not be keen on a regulatory budget designed to constrain the costs that an agency could impose on society. I am less certain about how they would feel about net benefit accounts but suspect that we would differ in the details. In particular, I would be more comfortable with accounts based on benefits and costs that are readily quantifiable, because they would be less easily manipulated.

Information markets—which can provide useful information on the likely outcome of an uncertain event—could be helpful in addressing problems associated with a regulatory budget and net benefit accounts. These markets can help provide a better understanding of the impact of government policies generally, and costs and benefits in particular.[295]

Finally, I would like to see more statutes advocating cost-benefit balancing as well as a statute that states that cost-benefit analysis should be allowed unless it is expressly prohibited by a particular law.[296] And, I would like to see agency analysis of costs and benefits that meets some basic criteria that are not being met now. These include quantification of benefits and costs to the extent reasonable, adequate consideration of alternatives, and use of standard values to ease comparison across regulations.[297] I am not sure that many of the critics would agree with this proposal.[298]

The bottom line is that the critics and I agree on several big policy issues, but we frequently disagree on the details.

VI

CONCLUSION

Scholars have made much progress over the past thirty years in understanding the economic impact of social regulation. In no small part, that progress is due to efforts to systematize knowledge, including the use of regulatory scorecards.

This monograph argues that, contrary to the critics' concerns, scorecards and economic analysis have made important contributions to the study of social regulation. These contributions include: first, illustrating that the cost-effectiveness of government regulations can vary substantially; second, showing that government regulation is inefficient in the sense that it is possible to get more for less, most notably in areas of environmental quality and life-saving investments; third, showing that a significant fraction of regulations are likely to fail a cost-benefit test based on the government's numbers and a significant fraction are likely to pass; and finally, illustrating serious problems with the quality of cost-benefit analyses done by the government in the area of social regulation.

The main studies that motivate this work, including a path-breaking study by Morrall, have come under intense scrutiny by the critics. Indeed, Parker goes so far as to suggest these studies are "shoddy."[299]

There are many ways to judge research, and the critics are certainly entitled to their opinions. I would like to offer an alternative viewpoint. Each of the studies to which Parker refers broke new ground. They should not be viewed as the last word on the subject, but rather closer to the first word. As such, it should not be surprising if each of them contains some errors.[300]

In judging these studies, one should ask several questions. First, do they ask important questions? I think even the critics would agree that they do. Indeed each study asks a variant of a very important question: Is it possible for society to get a higher return on its investment in social regulation?

Second, do these studies help shed light on a new research area? I think the answer is yes. Morrall was the first to suggest that cost-effectiveness of life-saving interventions could vary significantly across regulations. Tengs et al. was the first study to provide a comprehensive and accessible dataset on the estimated costs and effectiveness of life-saving interventions. Tengs and Graham were the first authors I know of to assess systematically the gains from changing the mix of life-saving interventions in the United States. My study was the first to provide a comprehensive analysis of economic information contained in government regulatory analyses.

Third, do these studies offer a reasonable approach and methodology for addressing the problem they define? While I think one can find defects in each of the analyses, each offers a reasonable and novel approach to the issues it addresses.

Fourth, are the major findings of these studies robust to changes in key assumptions or methodology? This is a harder question to answer. I cannot speak for the other studies. In the case of my study, I have done a considerable amount of sensitivity analysis prior to this monograph and partly in response to the critics. I think my results basically stand up with one exception. In retrospect, I should have been a bit more careful in dealing with the issue of presenting uncertainty in estimates. So, for example, my finding that less than half of the regulations would pass a narrow cost-benefit test, which seems to have so riled the critics, should have been stated more carefully. My belief now is that a significant number and a significant fraction of the regulations examined would not pass a cost-benefit test.[301]

Finally, will the major insights offered by these studies withstand the test of time? This is also a difficult question. My feeling is that Morrall's insight that cost-effectiveness varies tremendously across regulations has withstood the test of time. Similarly, I have no doubt that the basic insight of Tengs and Graham is correct concerning the possibility of achieving more of a given objective with fewer resources, in their case extending more lives for a given expenditure. Researchers are likely to continue to find substantial differences in cost-effectiveness in a variety of areas, including environmental regulation and life-saving investments.[302] While many future regulations are likely to pass a cost-benefit test, others are likely to fail, at least using current estimation methodologies and approaches. Retrospective analyses could change that finding.[303] If Congress implements dramatic changes in the regulatory process, however, that also could have a big impact on the economics of future social regulations.

The critics have made a useful contribution, but more needs to be done. Their mode of analysis tends to be critical of particular studies or groups of studies. Rather than simply providing critiques of particular papers, they may want to consider doing their own analyses of these issues. And if that is beyond their purview, they may want to encourage others to do so. I would be delighted if other academics attempted to do a serious replication of my initial research on a broader group of regulatory impact assessments or even on the same group of assessments. I have no doubt that such work would uncover new insights.[304]

Critics of regulatory scorecards and the economic analysis of social regulation have overplayed their hand. In particular, they have overstated the extent to which cost-benefit analysis and other quantitative tools are antiregulatory.[305] In principle, absolutely nothing is antiregulatory about these tools.[306] In practice, it is a stretch to suggest that the application of these tools in the main studies has been antiregulatory. Moreover, just because politicians use data in certain ways does not mean the underlying research is antiregulatory.

The critics need to appreciate that all social regulation is neither intrinsically good nor bad. In some situations, quantitative cost-benefit analysis and cost-effectiveness analysis will support regulations as they are; in others, they will suggest the need to change or eliminate regulation. The same holds true of regulatory programs as well as other policies aimed at improving health, safety, and the environment. Quantitative tools provide a useful method for systematically assessing some of the details as well as the bigger picture. The solution to legitimate concerns raised by the critics is not to eliminate the quantitative analysis, but to gain a deeper understanding of its strengths and weaknesses, and to use it wisely.

Despite my serious disagreement with many of the claims of the critics, I find myself in substantial agreement on a number of policy propositions. The points of agreement include: balancing quantitative and qualitative information in decision making; providing a better treatment of uncertainty; providing resources to investigate effects of regulation on different socioeconomic groups; increasing regulatory transparency; increasing funding to perform more retrospective analyses; and creating new institutional approaches for improving regulation.

One of the most intriguing features of Parker's critique of scorecards is what he leaves out. He does not critique, for example, the excellent work that some economists have done on the benefits of environmental regulation.[307] Yet this work certainly falls within the broad domain of scorecards. Nor does he critique my work assessing whether regulatory analyses covered important categories, such as quantifying benefits and costs.[308] Not surprisingly, the focus of the critics has been on results that do not serve their political ends, which appears to include giving agency regulators a larger say in regulatory decision making.

At the end of the day, the critics have spent a great deal of effort trying to discredit certain academics and their work. That they have made a valiant effort cannot be denied. They have shown that scholars should be careful in interpreting the findings from particular studies and that there are likely to be some mistakes in all studies with many numbers. But they have failed to show why scorecards or economic analysis of regulation should be abandoned. And they have failed to see how scorecards, in particular, have provided scholars and practitioners with useful insights into the policy process. Maybe they should consider abandoning the quest to banish scorecards that do not suit their needs and accept that economic analysis should be an important part of the regulatory policymaking process.

Notes

1. See Laurence H. Tribe, "Trial by Mathematics: Precision and Ritual in the Legal Process," *Harvard Law Review* 84 (1971): 1329.

2. See Daniel W. Bromley, "The Ideology of Efficiency: Searching for a Theory of Policy Analysis," *Journal of Environmental Economics and Management* 19 (1990), for critiques of economic policy analysis generally and cost-benefit analysis. See also Steven Kelman, "Cost-Benefit Analysis: An Ethical Critique," *Regulation* 5 (January–February 1981): 33–40, arguing that, in many instances, a certain decision may be right even though its benefits do not outweigh its costs, dollar values cannot be placed on nonmarketed benefits and costs, and devoting major resources to the generation of data for cost-benefit calculations is unjustified.

3. See Christopher C. DeMuth and Douglas H. Ginsburg, "White House Review of Agency Rulemaking," *Harvard Law Review* 99 (1986): 1075, for a defense of regulatory oversight that uses cost-benefit analysis. See also Kenneth Arrow et al., *Benefit-Cost Analysis in Environmental, Health, and Safety Regulation: A Statement of Principles* (Washington, D.C.: American Enterprise Institute, 1996), available at http://aei-brookings.org/publica tions/books/benefit_cost_analysis.pdf, for appropriate use of cost-benefit analysis in federal regulations (hereinafter *Benefit-Cost Principles*). See, e.g., Eric A. Posner, "Controlling Agencies with Cost-Benefit Analysis: A Positive Political Theory Perspective," *University of Chicago Law Review* 68 (2001), available at http://www.law.uchicago.edu/Lawecon/WkngPprs_ 101-25/119.EP.Controlling%20Agencies.pdf (accessed August 8, 2003), arguing that agencies and their supporters ought to endorse cost-benefit analysis, not resist it, and that cost-benefit analysis reduces the influence of interest groups. See, e.g., Amartya Sen, "The Discipline of Cost-Benefit Analysis,"

in *Cost-Benefit Analysis: Legal, Economic, and Philosophical Perspectives*, ed. Matthew D. Adler and Eric A. Posner (Chicago: University of Chicago Press, 2001), 114–15, stating, "However, even with these various foundational demands . . . the approach of cost-benefit analysis is rather permissive and can be adopted by many warring factions in the field of public decisions."

4. See Cass R. Sunstein, *Risk and Reason: Safety, Law, and the Environment* (Cambridge, UK: Cambridge University Press, 2002) (hereinafter *Risk and Reason*).

5. See Stephen Breyer, *Breaking the Vicious Circle: Toward Effective Risk Regulation* (Cambridge, Mass.: Harvard University Press, 1993) (hereinafter *Breaking the Vicious Circle*).

6. See, e.g., Robert W. Hahn and Cass R. Sunstein, "Regulatory Policy Takes Exciting New Tack," (September 2001), available at http://www.aei-brookings.org/policy/page.php?id=25 (accessed September 4, 2003), applauding the Office of Information and Regulatory Affairs' announcement and issue of "prompt letters" designed to encourage agencies to explore new areas in which regulation might deliver benefits that exceed costs.

7. See Cass R. Sunstein, *The Cost-Benefit State: The Future of Regulatory Protection* (Chicago: American Bar Association, 2002). See also Cass R. Sunstein, "The Cost-Benefit State," available at http://www.law.uchicago.edu/Publications/Working/WkngPprs%2026-50/39.sunstein.pdf (accessed September 4, 2003): "Gradually and in fits and starts, the American regulatory state is becoming a cost-benefit state. By this I mean that government regulation is increasingly assessed by asking whether the benefits of regulation justify the costs of regulation." See also Richard H. Pildes and Cass R. Sunstein, "Reinventing the Regulatory State," *University of Chicago Law Review* 32 (1995): 1.

8. See Robert W. Hahn, *Reviving Regulatory Reform: A Global Perspective* (Washington, D.C.: AEI-Brookings Joint Center for Regulatory Studies, 2000, 1): "But the concerns about regulation and the appropriate form of regulation extend beyond the United States. An array of developed and developing countries are now implementing and beginning to evaluate several regulatory reforms." See also Roger Noll, "Internationalizing Regulatory Reform," in *Comparative Disadvantages? Social Regulations and the Global Economy*, ed. Pietro Nivola (Washington, D.C.: The Brookings Institution Press, 1997), available at http://brookings.nap.edu/books/081576085X/ html/320.html# pagetop, focusing on the international aspects of regulatory policy.

9. See Lisa Heinzerling, "Regulatory Costs of Mythic Proportions," *Yale Law Journal* 107 (1998): 7 (hereinafter "Mythic Proportions"). See also Lisa

Heinzerling and Frank Ackerman, *Pricing the Priceless: Cost-Benefit Analysis of Environmental Protection* (Washington, D.C.: Georgetown Environmental Law and Policy Institute, 2002) (hereinafter *Pricing the Priceless*). See also Thomas O. McGarity, *Reinventing Rationality: The Role of Regulatory Analysis in the Federal Bureaucracy* (New York: Cambridge University Press, 1991) (hereinafter *Reinventing Rationality*).

10. See Richard W. Parker, "Grading the Government," *University of Chicago Law Review* 70 (October 2003): 1346, available at http://papers. ssrn.com/sol3/delivery.cfm/SSRN_ID370321_code030121140.pdf? abstractid=370321 (accessed January 2, 2004) (hereinafter "Grading the Government").

11. See *Report to Congress on the Costs and Benefits of Federal Regulations*, Office of Management and Budget (January 1999, 4), available at http://www.whitehouse.gov/omb/inforeg/costbenefitreport1998.pdf, stating, "The new estimates range from $170 billion to $230 billion in annual costs . . . for social, i.e., health, safety, and environmental regulation" (hereinafter *OMB 1998 Report*). See also *Stimulating Smarter Regulation: 2002 Report to Congress on the Costs and Benefits of Regulations and Unfunded Mandates on State, Local, and Tribal Entities*, Office of Management and Budget (2002, 6), available at http://www.whitehouse.gov/omb/inforeg/2002_report_to_congress.pdf (hereinafter *OMB 2002 Report*).

12. See *OMB 1998 Report*, 4, stating, "The new estimates range from . . . $260 billion to about $3.5 trillion in annual benefits for social, i.e., health, safety, and environmental regulation. Using the ranges to reflect the substantial uncertainty in the estimates, quantified (and monetized) net benefits could be as low as $30 billion, or as high as $3.3 trillion."

13. See Cass R. Sunstein, "Lives, Life-Years, and Willingness to Pay," *Columbia Law Review* 104 (2003), available at http://aei-brookings.org/admin/pdffiles/phprW.pdf, stating, "The hard question involves . . . how to monetize life-years, and here willingness-to-pay (WTP) is generally the place to begin." See also Lester Lave, "Benefit-Cost Analysis: Do the Benefits Exceed the Costs?" in *Risks, Costs, and Lives Saved*, ed. Robert W. Hahn (New York: Oxford University Press, 1996), discussing the fundamental merits of benefit-cost analysis and uncertainties in quantifying benefits and costs.

14. One argument is that the techniques themselves are seriously flawed. See Heinzerling and Ackerman, *Pricing the Priceless*, 33, stating, "Cost-benefit analysis is exceedingly time- and resource-intensive, and its flaws are so deep and so large that this time and these resources are wasted on it. . . . Cost-benefit analysis cannot overcome its fatal flaw: it is completely reliant on the impossible attempt to price the priceless values of life,

health, nature, and the future." A second argument is that the application of the techniques is particularly flawed. See Parker, "Grading the Government," 1355–56.

15. See section II for a formal definition of scorecards.

16. A cost-effective regulation can achieve a given objective at least cost. Moreover, if one regulation costs $1 to reduce a ton of sulfur dioxide and a second regulation costs $100, the first would be more cost-effective. A regulation is said to offer positive net benefits if the difference between the total benefits and the total costs is positive.

17. The costs are probably better interpreted as the expected cost per life saved. Generally, when I provide information on costs and benefits in this monograph, they should be interpreted in terms of expected or average values unless noted otherwise. For a seminal analysis on the costs of various risk-reducing regulations per life saved, see John F. Morrall, "A Review of the Record," *Regulation* (November–December 1986): 25–34, table 4, stating, "The most obvious implication of these figures is that the range of cost-effectiveness among rules is enormous" (hereinafter "Review of the Record").

18. See Tammy Tengs et al., "Five-Hundred Life-Saving Interventions and Their Cost-Effectiveness," *Risk Analysis* 15 (1995): 369, 369–90, finding that there is enormous variation in the cost of saving one year of life, that these differences exist both within and between categories, and that where there are investment inequalities, more lives could be saved by shifting resources (hereinafter "Life-Saving Interventions").

19. The term *lives saved* refers to reductions in mortality risk or statistical lives saved, not to identifiable lives saved. See W. Kip Viscusi, *Fatal Tradeoffs: Public and Private Responsibilities for Risk* (New York: Oxford University Press, 1992), for discussion of value of statistical life.

20. See Tengs et al.,"Life-Saving Interventions," 377, 373.

21. In the case of cars, for example, the government has mandated safety standards for bumpers, seatbelts, and the center brake light in automobiles.

22. See Breyer, *Breaking the Vicious Circle*, cited in note 5.

23. See Tammy O. Tengs and John D. Graham, "The Opportunity Costs of Haphazard Social Investments in Life-Saving," in *Risks, Costs, and Lives Saved*, ed. Robert W. Hahn, 167–204 (New York: Oxford University Press, 1996) (hereinafter "Opportunity Costs"), finding that retaining the present pattern of investments in the 185 life-saving interventions considered results in the loss of $31.1 billion, 636,000 life-years, or 60,200 lives every year. Tengs and Graham also suggest that estimates of the cost per life saved should be transformed to cost per life-year by considering the

average number of years of life saved when a premature death is averted. For example, when the death of a forty-year-old who would have lived to age seventy-seven is averted, thirty-seven years of life are saved.

24. See Robert W. Hahn, *Reviving Regulatory Reform: A Global Perspective* (Washington, D.C.: AEI-Brookings Joint Center for Regulatory Studies, 2000), 63 (hereinafter Government Numbers II). See section III, here, for a more detailed discussion of these issues and findings. Within the text of this piece, *the study* refers to chapter 3 in Government Numbers II. *The main studies* refer to Hahn's Government Numbers II, Morrall's "Review of the Record," Tengs et al.'s "Life-Saving Interventions," and Tengs and Graham's "Opportunity Costs."

25. See Robert W. Hahn, "Regulatory Reform: What Do the Government's Numbers Tell Us?," in *Risks, Costs, and Lives Saved*, ed. Robert W. Hahn, 237 (New York: Oxford University Press, 1996), "In Mexico, a dollar expenditure on a life-saving activity is about thirty times as effective as spending that amount on a recent average federal regulation; in the low-income countries it is over 1,500 times as effective; and in the middle-income countries, it is almost 300 times as effective." (hereinafter Government Numbers I). *My early study* refers to Government Numbers I. *My studies* refer to Government Numbers I and Government Numbers II.

26. See Hahn, Government Numbers II, 63, cited in note 24: "My analysis of the impact of federal regulatory activities on the economy shows that . . . less than half of final regulations pass a strict benefit-cost test." See the discussion in section III.

27. See Parker, "Grading the Government," 13, available at http://papers. ssrn.com/sol3/delivery.cfm/SSRN_ID370321_code030121140.pdf?abstrac tid=370321 (last visited January 2, 2004), "Whether or not single-rule cost-benefit analysis is a useful enterprise in practice (an issue on which this Article takes no position), it is clear that numerical scorecards are inherently, and fatally, flawed even when judged by the standards of their own discipline." See Parker, "Grading the Government," 1356: "Scorecards cannot be salvaged. They should simply be abandoned."

28. *Social regulation* is defined as environmental, health, and safety regulation for purposes of this piece. See, e.g., Paul Joskow and Roger Noll, "Regulation in Theory and Practice: A Current Overview," in *Studies in Public Regulation*, ed. Gary Fromm (Cambridge, Mass.: The MIT Press, 1981).

29. See Parker and other critics for criticisms.

30. See McGarity, *Reinventing Rationality*. See also Heinzerling, "Mythic Proportions." See also Parker, "Grading the Government."

31. See Center for Progressive Regulation (CPR), at http://www.pro gressiveregulation.org/: "The Center for Progressive Regulation seeks to improve the quality of public debate on matters of environmental, health, and safety policy. . . . CPR is a 'virtual' organization, utilizing the capabilities of the internet to link together individuals from throughout the country who are interested in the constructive role that sensible government regulation can play in improving environmental quality, public health and safety for ourselves, future generations, and the entire planet." For the Center for Progressive Regulation's perspective on cost-benefit analysis, see http://www. progressiveregulation.org/perspectives/costbenefit.html: "Two features of cost-benefit analysis distinguish it from other approaches to evaluating the advantages and disadvantage of environmentally protective regulations: the translation of lives, health, and the natural environment into monetary terms, and the discounting of harms to human health and the environment that are expected to occur in the future. CPR believes that these features of cost-benefit analysis make it a terrible way to make decisions about environmental protection, for both intrinsic and practical reasons. . . . Cost-benefit analysis is exceedingly time- and resource-intensive, and its flaws are so deep and so large that this time and these resources are wasted on it."

32. See Morrall, "Review of the Record," cited in note 17. See Tengs et al., "Life-Saving Interventions," note 18. See Tengs and Graham, "Opportunity Costs," note 23. For studies on the costs and benefits of regulation using government regulatory impact analyses, see Hahn, Government Numbers II, note 24, and Government Numbers I, note 25. For a definition of regulatory impact analysis, see Appendix C: OMB Draft Guidelines for the Conduct of Regulatory Analysis and the Format of Accounting Statements, *Federal Register* 68 (February 3, 2003): 5513–14, available at http://www.whitehouse.gov/omb/fedreg/2003draft_cost-benefit_rpt.pdf (hereinafter *OMB 2003 Draft Report*): "Regulatory Analysis is a tool regulatory agencies use to anticipate and evaluate the likely consequences of their actions. It provides a formal way of organizing the evidence on the key effects—good and bad—of the various alternatives that should be considered in developing regulations. The motivation is to (1) learn if the benefits of an action are likely to justify the costs or (2) discover which of various possible alternatives would be most cost-effective. By choosing actions that maximize net benefits, agencies direct resources to their most efficient use." See also Hahn, Government Num-bers II, 84, cited in note 24, n. 4, for a definition of regulatory impact analyses and major regulations: "Agencies have produced RIAs for every regulation since Reagan's Executive Order 12291, issued in 1981. An RIA includes

the agency's estimates of the benefits and costs of the regulation in addition to other information designed in the executive order. Reagan's order required agencies to produce an RIA for each proposed and final "major" rule, defined generally as a rule with an estimated annual impact on the economy of $100 million or more. President Clinton's Executive Order 12866, issued in 1993, changed the term *regulatory impact analysis* to *economic analysis* and the term *major* to *economically significant* but otherwise did not significantly change the RIA requirement. I use *regulatory impact analysis* throughout this chapter because analysts use the term more frequently than *economic analysis*."

33. See Parker, "Grading the Government," 1349. See also Heinzerling, "Mythic Proportions"; Heinzerling and Ackerman, *Pricing the Priceless*; and Sidney A. Shapiro and Robert L. Glicksman, *Risk Regulation at Risk: Restoring a Pragmatic Balance* (Palo Alto: Stanford University Press, 2003) (hereinafter *Pragmatic Balance*).

34. Parker defines *scorecards* as follows: "Regulatory scorecards are a sub-species of cost-benefit analysis. While the typical cost-benefit analysis devotes hundreds of pages to a narrative describing the costs and benefits of a single project or rule, scorecards reduce these hundreds of pages to a few summary statistics—costs, benefits, net benefits and/or cost-per-life saved. Scorecards then tabulate these summary statistics across scores of rules in order to generate what appears to be a concise, precise, and comprehensive picture of the cost-benefit rationality of programs, agencies, and regulations overall." Parker, "Grading the Government," 1348–49.

35. See Parker, "Grading the Government," 1347: "The remarkable ascendancy of the anti-regulatory movement derives from two main empirical sources. One is a stream of well-publicized 'horror stories' of government zealotry and caprice. . . . The obvious shortcomings of anecdotes as vehicles of proof have given rise to a group of broader studies that have largely supplanted anecdotes as the leading source of skepticism. These studies have yet to be recognized as a formal genre. I will call them 'regulatory scorecards.'"

36. See Parker, "Grading the Government," 1404: ". . . rule analyses are not and cannot be what scorecardists implicitly assume they are and must be: final declarations of exactly what one will find at the end of the process."

37. Parker makes the claim that scorecardists implicitly assume that rule analyses are final declarations of exactly what one will find at the end of the process. However, he provides no evidence proving this case. In fact,

scorecards assume something close to the opposite, namely that rule analyses are incomplete. See Government Numbers II, 34: "Scholars have found that the information provided in the RIA is often not complete and that the level of detail and analytical sophistication varies across agencies and types of regulations." My scorecards did not claim that rule analyses were final declarations.

38. For a discussion of the benefits of scorecards, see section IV. See also figure 1, showing how infrequently agencies monetize benefits in their regulatory analyses.

39. See A. Myrick Freeman, "Environmental Policy since Earth Day I: What Have We Gained?" *Journal of Economic Perspectives* 16, no. 1 (2002): 125–46.

40. See Thomas D. Hopkins, *Costs of Regulation: Filling the Gaps*, 1–38, Regulatory Information Service Center, table 1 (August 1992). Table 1 shows the annualized regulatory costs by type of regulation from 1977 to 2000. The table reveals that the costs of environmental and process regulation increase over time and, in 2000, process regulation and environmental regulation cost more than all other types of regulation, costing \$221 billion and \$178 billion, respectively, in 1991 dollars.

41. See Robert W. Hahn and John A. Hird, "The Costs and Benefits of Regulation: Review and Synthesis," *Yale Journal of Regulation* 8 (1990): 233 (hereinafter "Costs and Benefits"). This study was motivated by several earlier studies, including works by Weidenbaum and DeFina, and Litan and Nordhaus. See Murray L. Weidenbaum and Robert DeFina, *The Cost of Federal Regulation of Economic Activity* (Washington, D.C.: American Enterprise Institute, 1978). See also Robert E. Litan and William D. Nordhaus, *Reforming Federal Regulation* (New Haven: Yale University Press, 1983).

42. See Robert W. Hahn and Cass R. Sunstein, "A New Executive Order for Improving Federal Regulation? Deeper and Wider Cost Benefit Analysis," *University of Pennsylvania Law Review* 150 (2002): 1519, table 4.

43. This is not to suggest that the critics have focused solely on these studies. For criticisms of Hopkins's scorecard on costs of regulations, see Shapiro and Glicksman, *Pragmatic Balance*, 74.

44. See Joseph Stiglitz, *Economics of the Public Sector* (Palo Alto: Stanford University Press, 2000), 273. Stiglitz writes that discounting comes from the premise that people prefer one dollar today to one dollar tomorrow.

45. See Paul R. Portney and John P. Weyant, eds., *Discounting and Intergenerational Equity* (Washington, D.C.: Resources for the Future,1999), 6–7: *"With one exception, every chapter in this volume suggests that it is*

appropriate—indeed essential—to discount future benefits and costs at some positive rate. . . . Analysts may want to use different discount rates depending on the period over which they are calculating net present values. . . . The possibility of nonconstant discounting is suggested by a growing number of studies in which individuals' discount rates are inferred either from their observed behavior in actual markets or their responses to hypothetical questions about their attitudes toward risk, life-saving behavior, or the life-saving activities of government."

46. When I use the terms *lives saved, life-years saved,* and related terms throughout this monograph, I am referring to "statistical lives," not identifiable people in the sense that we know the name of the person before the fact who will be saved in a particular instance. Moreover, when I use a number, such as 50,000 life-years saved, that number would refer to an estimate, usually the expected value or average. For an in-depth discussion of the difference between statistical lives and identified lives, see Viscusi, *Fatal Tradeoffs,* 20, cited in note 19: "The valuation of identified lives involving 0–1 probabilities of life or death will, of course, be quite different from the valuation of statistical lives. . . . From an economic standpoint, the statistical life valuation is the one correct approach to valuing statistical lives. . . . Suppose that improved water treatment facilities will reduce the rate of a fatal form of cancer by 1/10,000 for a municipality of 20,000, so that on average two lives will be saved. Suppose that we knew in fact that two lives would be saved, but we did not know whose they would be."

47. Suppose we have a simple two-period model, where costs of a regulation are $1 and occur in the first period, and benefits of the regulation are not realized until the second period, when they are worth $1.05. If we use a 5-percent annual discount rate, the value in the first period of benefits received in the second period is $1, or $1.05/(1 + 0.05). Since costs equal $1 in the first period and benefits equal $1 in the first period, net benefits in the first period equal $0. However, if we use a 0-percent discount rate, the value in the first period of $1.05 of benefits received in the second period will be $1.05. With costs of $1 incurred in the first period, net benefits will equal $1.05 − $1, or $0.05, using a 0-percent discount rate. See Michael Parkin, *Economics* (Boston: Addison-Wesley Publishing, 1996), 198–99.

48. See Hahn, Government Numbers I, 233, cited in note 25, table 10-6 (illustrating the impact of varying the discount rate from 3 percent to 5 percent on the net benefits of final rules).

49. See Parker, "Grading the Government," 30: "Hahn's base case employs a discount rate of 5 percent which is well above the 'consumption'

rate of interest (2–3 percent) that many economists believe is the appropriate rate for discounting future benefits to consumers in an open economy."

50. Parker claims that the consumption rate is appropriate, citing a monograph by Arrow et al. in which I was a coauthor. Although the consumption rate may be appropriate under some circumstances, there are other legitimate perspectives on the discount rate issue. I think that one must look at other factors, including the displacement of investment resulting from regulation, which means one must look at the cost of capital. Portney and Weyant, summarizing the findings of a workshop of distinguished economists on the subject, note that the participants agreed "not only that it is appropriate to discount benefits and costs for the purposes of making present value comparisons, but also that the discount rate to use should be one that reflects the *opportunity cost of capital*" (emphasis added). Portney and Weyant, *Discounting and Intergenerational Equity*, 7, cited in note 45. There-fore, it is quite reasonable, in my view, to use a rate that ranges between 3 and 7 percent, as I did. The consumption rate would reflect the low end of the range and the opportunity cost of capital would reflect the high end.

51. See Economic Analysis of Federal Regulations under Executive Order 12866 ("Best Practices Guidelines"), section III.A.§3 (1996), available at http://www.whitehouse.gov/omb/inforeg/riaguide.html (hereinafter Best Practices I): "The basic guidance for regulatory and other analyses is provided in OMB Circular A-94. The discount rate specified in that guidance is intended to be an approximation of the opportunity cost of capital, which is the before-tax rate of return to incremental private investment. The Circular A-94 rate, which was revised in 1992 based on an extensive review and public comment, reflects the rates of return on low yielding forms of capital, such as housing, as well as the higher rates of return yielded by corporate capital. This average rate currently is estimated to be 7 percent in real terms (i.e., after adjusting for inflation)." Regarding adjustments to the discount rate over time, OMB's "Best Practices Guidelines" states: "In general, the discount rate should not be adjusted to account for the uncertainty of future benefits and costs." See Best Practices I, section III.A.§3: Discounting.

52. See *Informing Regulatory Decisions: 2003 Report to Congress on the Costs and Benefits of Federal Regulations and Unfunded Mandates on State, Local, and Tribal Entities*, Office of Management and Budget, Circular A-4, available at http://www.whitehouse.gov/omb/inforeg/2003_cost-ben_final_rpt.pdf: "For regulatory analysis, you should provide estimates of net benefits using both 7 percent and 3 percent. . . . Some have argued, however, that it

is ethically impermissible to discount utility of future generations. . . . Even under this approach, it would still be correct to discount future costs and consumption benefits, although perhaps at a lower rate than for intergenerational analysis. . . . Estimates of the discount rate appropriate in this case made in the 1990s ranged from 1 to 3 percent per annum. . . . If you choose to use a lower discount rate for intergenerational analysis, you should still be sure to show the calculated net benefits using discount rates of 3 and 7 percent as well." See also EPA SAB 812 Report.

53. See Heinzerling and Ackerman, *Pricing the Priceless*, 1–2: "[T]he use of discounting systematically and improperly downgrades the importance of environmental regulation. While discounting makes sense in comparing alternative *financial* investments, it cannot reasonably be used to make a choice between preventing noneconomic harms to present generations and preventing similar harms to future generations. Nor can discounting reasonably be used even to make a choice between harms to the current generation; the choice between preventing an automobile fatality and a cancer death should not turn on prevailing rates of return on financial investments." See also Shapiro and Glicksman, *Pragmatic Balance*, 84–85, 111, also questioning discounting as irrational and compiling regulatory scorecards employing no discount rate at all. See, e.g., Heinzerling, "Mythic Proportions," B.1., n. 231, calculating risks and costs with a zero discount rate.

54. Shapiro and Glicksman, *Pragmatic Balance*, 118.

55. It would pay to defer investments in life saving or any other benefits, for that matter, indefinitely.

56. For a more in-depth critique of Heinzerling's approach, see John J. Donahue, "Why We Should Discount the Views of Those Who Discount Discounting," *Yale Law Journal* 108 (1998): 1905: "But if it is appropriate to discount in the traditional cost-benefit analysis, then it is also appropriate for Morrall to have done so in his cost-per-life-saved approach. The two are mathematically equivalent. Heinzerling improperly draws rhetorical support for her position—that we should not 'discount' lives saved in the future—by invoking the layman's notion of discounting as somehow devaluing future lives, rather than the analyst's conception of it as a tool to convert all costs and benefits into a single present value calculation. Yet it is only the happenstance that Morrall employed a cost-per-life-saved calculation that enables Heinzerling to marshal the rhetorical opposition. In this sense, the rhetoric about 'discounting lives' is a mere distraction, since traditional cost-benefit analysis would simply be discounting dollars." See also Emmett B. Keeler and Shan Cretin, "Discounting of Life-Saving and Other Nonmonetary Effects," *Management Science* 29, no. 3

(1983), showing that using a lower discount rate for benefits than for costs leads "to some peculiar, even absurd consequences." The paper also shows that the failure to discount benefits implies that programs are always improved by delay, as long as the ability to produce nonmonetary benefits does not diminish too quickly over time. Finally, it argues that the discount rate for monetary and nonmonetary benefits should be equal when hard-to-monetize benefits such as life-saving are involved.

57. See Donahue, "Why We Should Discount the Views," 1905, cited in note 56: "[D]iscounting is appropriate in that, if invested, our resources are expected to grow at that rate, so that if we forego spending and invest the money instead, we can save more lives in the future with the amount foregone today."

58. See Donahue, "Why We Should Discount the Views," 1904: "Since 'both economic efficiency and intergenerational equity require that benefits and costs experienced in future years be given less weight in decision-making than those experienced today,' the process of discounting future costs and benefits to current dollars has become standard. Expressing all costs and benefits in current dollars should yield valuable information about the wisdom of adopting a particular proposal." See also Best Practices I. See also Arrow et al., "Benefit-Cost Principles."

59. For further discussion of the appropriate range of discount rates and sensitivity analyses using an expanded range of discount rates, see section III. Increasing the range does not affect the key conclusions.

60. See Parker, "Grading the Government," 1364: "Hahn, however, follows OMB in defining 'major rules' as those that cost more than $100 million per year to comply with. This filter effectively excludes from the database the most cost-effective interventions of all: interventions which yield (or would, if adopted, yield) major benefits without imposing major costs. The result is an in-built sampling bias against regulation. An equal or greater source of bias is found in the fact that both Morrall and Hahn focus on rules, actual or proposed. They choose not to examine rules that were never issued but would be cost-effective if they had been. . . . This means that under-regulation can be just as inefficient—in the sense of producing a misallocation of resources—as over-regulation. By systematically excluding all cases of under-regulation, Hahn and Morrall introduce yet a further skew towards a finding of over-regulation."

61. I identify general conclusions from the scorecard literature that I think are robust later in this monograph. See discussion in section IV: "In Support of Regulatory Scorecards and the Economic Analysis of Regulation."

62. See John F. Morrall, "Saving Lives: A Review of the Record," *Journal of Risk and Uncertainty* 27 (2003): 33, table 3, available at http://www.aei-brookings.org/publications/ abstract.php?pid=354 (hereinafter "Saving Lives"). Table 3 in Morrall's paper directly responds to concerns raised by the critics by listing several regulatory opportunities. See also Morrall, "Saving Lives," 19: "In 1999 FDA proposed to reduce the intake of trans fatty acids by requiring labeling. . . . In 2003, FDA proposed requiring bar codes for drugs and biologic products. OMB also sent a prompt letter to promote AEDs in the workplace. A fourth suggestion is to promote the increased intake of omega-3 fatty acids, which are primarily found in dark meat fish."

63. For an example illustrating OMB's identification of regulatory opportunities that are either efficient or cost-effective, see OIRA's website, at http://www.whitehouse.gov/omb/inforeg/regpol.html#rr: "The purpose of the prompt letter is to suggest an issue that OMB believes is worthy of agency priority. Rather than being sent in response to the agency's submission of a draft rule for OIRA review, a 'prompt' letter is sent on OMB's initiative and contains a suggestion for how the agency could improve its regulations." See also Robert W. Hahn and Cass R. Sunstein, "Regulatory Oversight Takes Exciting New Tack" (2001), available at http://www.aei-brookings.org/policy/page.php?id=25: "These 'prompt letters' are an exceedingly important development. For far too long, the idea of cost-benefit analysis has been wrongly associated with mindless opposition to regulation. To be sure, an exploration of costs and benefits often shows that regulation cannot be justified. But cost-benefit analyses can show, and have shown, that government action is worthwhile—and indeed that government should do more. Such analyses helped encourage policymakers to get the lead out of gasoline and protect the ozone layer."

64. See Tengs et al., "Life-Saving Interventions," 369, cited in note 18: "We report cost-effectiveness ratios for more than 500 life-saving interventions across all sectors of American society."

65. See Hahn, Government Numbers II, 32: "This chapter provides the most comprehensive assessment to date of the impact of federal regulatory activities on the economy. The analysis is based on a review of all rules with regulatory impact analyses, or RIAs, that I could locate from 1981 through mid-1996, a total of 168 final and proposed rules."

66. See Parker, "Grading the Government," 1364.

67. See Si Kyung Seong and John Mendeloff, *Assessing the Accuracy of OSHA's Projections of the Benefits of New Safety Standards* (2003), 23, available at http://www.aei-brookings.org/publications/abstract.php?pid=357, suggesting that OSHA prepared the most-accurate cost projections for its most

expensive safety standards or major rules and the least-accurate for its cheapest standards, which fell in the minor rules category. The category of minor rules is one of many areas that could benefit from further study. We still know very little about a number of areas, including the economics of major rules from independent agencies, regulatory guidance, and cost-effective or efficient regulatory opportunities that do not make it to the proposed or final rule-making stage. We are even missing economic analyses of many major rules. The fact that we know little about certain parts of the puzzle should not preclude us from studying other parts, where we can learn something. I think that such learning is a critical part of the scientific endeavor.

68. See Parker, "Grading the Government," 1364.

69. The OMB sometimes negotiates informally with the agencies over which rules to consider major.

70. See Stephen Breyer, *Breaking the Vicious Circle*, arguing that agencies suffer from "tunnel vision."

71. See ibid., 11.

72. For an interesting proposal about obtaining estimates of ex-post net benefits through the use of markets, see Michael Abramowicz, "Information Markets, Administrative Decisionmaking, and Predictive Cost-Benefit Analysis," *University of Chicago Law Review* 71 (August 2003): 933–1015, available at http://www.aei-brookings.org/publications/abstract.php?pid=370.

73. See *Report to Congress on the Costs and Benefits of Federal Regulations*, Office of Management and Budget (1998), 8, 18, available at http://www. whitehouse.gov/omb/inforeg/costbenefitreport1998.pdf, for an early OMB report that discusses the need for retrospective analysis: "In the ordinary course, therefore, the best estimates of the costs and benefits of regulation are likely to be retrospective studies done by individuals who do not have vested interests, but do have reputations as objective analysts to uphold. . . . Where we can make direct comparisons between prospective and retrospective analyses, we find that both costs and benefits were sometimes overestimated by prospective studies. In other instances, costs were underestimated." See also Robert W. Hahn and Robert N. Stavins, "Economic Incentives for Environmental Protection: Integrating Theory and Practice," *American Economic Review* 82, no. 2 (1992): 464 (hereinafter "Economic Incentives").

74. See Hahn, Government Numbers I, 239: "This analysis uses as its main source of data regulatory analyses that were done before the enactment of regulations. It would be useful to compare those analyses with what actually occurred to determine likely biases in the estimates. That is a

laborious exercise, but one that could identify systematic biases associated with doing prospective analyses of proposed policies." See also Hahn, Government Numbers II, cited in note 24: "In addition, agencies could use retrospective studies of actual impacts to complement prospective studies. Such analyses would provide a better assessment of actual benefits and costs than agencies currently provide and would help agencies improve prospective analytical techniques."

75. See Tengs et al., "Life-Saving Interventions," 372, cited in note 18: "These interventions are best thought of as opportunities for investment. While they may offer insight into the actual investments in life-saving, the cost-effectiveness of possible and actual investments are not equivalent. Work on the economic efficiency of actual expenditures is in progress."

76. See Parker, "Grading the Government," 1367: "Morrall and Hahn likewise describe their findings as actual costs and benefits when, in fact, Morrall and Hahn derive their data exclusively from regulatory impact statements long before the rule in question took effect. Confusing predictions with actual results has two deleterious effects. First, it creates a bogus appearance of precision which renders the scorecards highly quotable—and fundamentally misleading." However, never do I claim that my findings result from actual costs and benefits. Rather, I state that I am using the government's numbers in the RIAs. See also Heinzerling and Ackerman, *Pricing the Priceless*, 28, cited in note 53: "There is also a tendency, as a matter of practice, to overestimate the costs of regulations in advance of their implementation. . . . One study found that costs estimated in advance of regulation were more than twice actual costs in 11 out of 12 cases. Another study found that advance cost estimates were more than 25 percent too low in only 3 of the 28 cases." For a critique of Heinzerling and Ackerman's argument, see Winston Harrington, Richard D. Morgenstern, and Peter Nelson, "On the Accuracy of Regulatory Cost Estimates," *Journal of Policy Analysis and Management* 19, no. 2 (2000): 297 (hereinafter "Regulatory Cost Estimates"): "This study compares ex ante estimates of the direct costs of individual regulations to ex post assessments of the same regulations. For total costs the results support conventional wisdom, namely that the costs of regulations tend to be overestimated. This is true for 14 of the 28 rules in the data set discussed, while for only 3 rules were the ex ante estimates too low. For unit costs, however, the story is quite different. At least for EPA and OSHA rules, unit cost estimates are often accurate, and even when they are not, overestimation of abatement costs occurs about as often as underestimation."

77. Even when ex-post estimates are done, they may be subject to great uncertainty. See A. Denny Ellerman et al., *Emissions Trading under the U.S. Acid Rain Program: Evaluation of Compliance Costs and Allowance Market Performance* (Cambridge, Mass.: The MIT Press, 1997), 2–66.

78. That is, I do not think we know enough to assess the intrinsic bias in cost or benefits relative to some objective measure of these items. For further discussion of the importance of retrospective analyses, see Hahn, Government Numbers I, 63, cited in note 25.

79. For an interesting paper that compares ex-ante and ex-post estimates of the economic impacts of regulation, see Harrington et al., "Regulatory Cost Estimates," 314, cited in note 76: "For federal rules the overestimation of total costs is often due to errors in the quantity of required emission reductions which, in turn, is driven by both baseline and compliance issues. In these cases, the ex ante overestimate of total costs implies an overestimate of total benefits (pollution reductions)." Reviewing more than two dozen regulations with *ex-ante* and detailed *ex-post* cost estimates, the authors found that, although the costs of regulations tend to be overestimated, such instances also tended to imply overestimation of benefits. See also Winston Harrington, Richard D. Morgenstern, and Peter Nelson, "Predicting the Costs of Environmental Regulations: How Accurate Are Regulators' Estimates?" *Environment* 41, no. 7 (1999): 44: "Society may pay less, but it also gets less. Moreover, per unit abatement cost estimates were generally accurate, with overestimation occurring about as often as underestimation." See also Si Kyung Seong and John Mendeloff, *Assessing the Accuracy of OSHA's Projections of the Benefits of New Safety Standards*, cited in note 67. For six safety standards issued by OSHA since 1990, this paper compares OSHA's projections of their impact on fatalities with actual fatality changes and explains the reasons for the differences.

80. See Heinzerling and Ackerman, *Pricing the Priceless*, 27–28: "Cost-benefit studies of regulations focus on quantified benefits of the proposed action and generally ignore other, non-quantified health and environmental benefits. . . . In practice, however, unquantified values are often forgotten, or even denigrated, once all the numbers have been crunched." See also Lisa Heinzerling, "The Perils of Precision," *Environmental Law Institute* (1998). See, e.g., Shapiro and Glicksman, *Pragmatic Balance*, 103.

81. Parker expresses concern about cost omissions also. See Parker, "Grading the Government," 1405: "The culpability of scorecards is found, not in their failure to detect previously unidentified costs and benefits, but in their omission of costs and benefits which the agencies identify and describe narratively, but do not pretend to be able to quantify or

monetize. . . . Could better scorecard methodology avoid such problems? The answer is clearly no." I am concerned about omissions of costs and benefits but do not feel that is a reason not to have good quantitative analysis inform the decision-making process. Furthermore, contrary to Parker's assertion, different types of scorecards can account for unquantified benefits and costs.

82. See Arrow et al., "Benefit-Cost Principles," 10: "A common critique of benefit-cost analysis is that it does not emphasize factors that are not easily quantified or monetized. That critique has merit. There are two principal ways to address it: first, quantify as many factors as are reasonable and quantify or characterize the relevant uncertainties; and second, give due consideration to factors that defy quantification but are thought to be important."

83. See Hahn, Government Numbers I, 33 cited in note 24, for objectives of my "main study": "After assessing the quality of various agencies' estimates of the benefits and costs of regulation, I present the key analytical results concerning the net benefits. I also estimate the cost-effectiveness of selected regulations. Then, I evaluate the relationship between the wording of statutory requirements for economic analysis and the efficiency of regulations and discuss whether regulatory impact analyses have improved the regulatory process. Finally, I conclude with suggestions for further regulatory reform." See Tengs et al., "Life-Saving Interventions," 369, cited in note 18, for the objectives of Tengs et al.'s major study (gathering information on the cost-effectiveness of life-saving interventions in the United States from publicly available economic analyses). See Morrall, "Review of the Record," 25, cited in note 17: "Reducing health and safety risks has been a top priority of federal regulation for almost two decades, yet there is little systematic information describing the kinds of risks the government has chosen to regulate or the effectiveness of these interventions. This article is a modest attempt to fill the gap—I hope no more than a first step." Qualitative factors could be introduced in a variety of ways in future studies. See discussion, section IV, "In Support of Regulatory Scorecards and the Economic Analysis of Regulation." I could introduce qualitative factors to some of the scorecards by (1) adding qualitative issue discussion next to each regulation, (2) using a method to quantify key qualitative factors, and (3) getting expert judgment on the importance or monetary value of these qualitative factors.

84. This table is another example of a scorecard. The critics ignore this type of scorecard, which reveals the quality of agency analyses. See table 1. The scorecard includes 121 final rules and 47 proposed rules. The row

entitled, "Benefits or cost savings assessed" includes assessment of fatal and nonfatal human health benefits from reduction in the risk of cancer, heart disease, lead poisoning, and car, fire, and workplace accidents. The category also includes assessment of benefits from pollution reduction and any other benefits or cost savings that the agency quantified or monetized. See Hahn, Government Numbers II, 36, table 3-1.

85. See Robert W. Hahn et al., "Assessing Regulatory Impact Analyses: The Failure of Agencies to Comply with Executive Order 12,866," *Harvard Journal of Law and Public Policy* 23, no. 3 (2000): 859 (hereinafter "Assessing Regulatory Impact Analyses"), suggesting that the impact of RIAs has fallen short of the expectations of regulatory reform advocates in part because agencies do not fully comply with the OMB's guidelines: "The Article also offers specific suggestions for improving the quality of RIAs, which will in turn improve the allocation of regulatory resources." See also the discussion in section IV, "In Support of Regulatory Scorecards and the Economic Analysis of Regulation."

86. See Parker, "Grading the Government," 13: "[A]lthough scholars to date have treated regulatory scorecards as simply another form of cost-benefit analysis, this Article will demonstrate that, in fact, regulatory scorecards represent a distinct sub-species of cost-benefit analysis which inherently violates the basic rules that govern such analysis. Whether or not a single-rule cost-benefit analysis is a useful enterprise in practice (an issue on which this Article takes no position), it is clear that numerical scorecards are inherently, and fatally, flawed even when judged by the standards of their own discipline. Scorecards cannot be salvaged. They should simply be abandoned."

87. See Parker, "Grading the Government," 1355: "Part II examines a group of equally serious shortcomings which could not have been avoided because they are inherent in the enterprise of compiling numerical scorecards. First and foremost, regulatory scorecards ignore virtually all benefits that are not quantified and/or monetized—thereby excluding most environmental benefits, many health benefits, and all intangible benefits ranging from avoidance of pain and suffering or familial and societal disruption to the promotion of a public sense of security, fairness, confidence in markets, etc."

88. See the discussion in section IV, "In Support of Regulatory Scorecards and the Economic Analysis of Regulation."

89. See Morrall, "Review of the Record," 30, table 4, for a table showing the cost of various risk-reducing regulations per life saved. A column specifying important qualitative factors could be added to this table. See also Morrall, "Saving Lives," 31, table 1.

90. See Heinzerling and Ackerman, *Pricing the Priceless*, 33: "Nor is it useful to keep cost-benefit analysis around as a kind of regulatory tag-along, providing information that regulators may find 'interesting' even if not decisive. Cost-benefit analysis is exceedingly time and resource-intensive, and its flaws are so deep and so large that this time and these resources are wasted on it."

91. The Center for Progressive Regulation, to which many of the critics belong, believes in developing policies to protect human health and the environment without relying on cost-benefit analysis. To do this, CPR "believes that it is useful to distinguish between decisions about means and decisions about ends. CPR believes that it has sometimes proved useful to consult economic analysis in order to develop the most cost-effective *means* for carrying out a predetermined regulatory policy. Emissions trading programs, for example, came about in this way. CPR does not, however, believe that it is useful to try to set the *ends* of environmental policy through economic analysis." CPR does not provide an alternative that would improve regulatory outcomes or the regulatory process. For example, how does one illustrate and analyze the benefits and costs of a regulatory policy in order to increase transparency and accountability? Cost-benefit analysis is the only viable method I know of. Moreover, cost-effectiveness analysis already provides insights into the most cost-effective means for carrying out a predetermined regulatory policy.

92. See, e.g., Richard D. Morgenstern, ed., *Economic Analyses at EPA: Assessing Regulatory Impact* (Washington, D.C.: Resources for the Future, 1997), and Morrall, "Saving Lives."

93. I am not aware of any systematic empirical studies in the regulatory area that measure the importance of qualitative and quantitative factors in regulatory decision making. For a study on the importance of analysis, see Scott Farrow, "Improving Regulatory Performance: Does Executive Oversight Matter?" AEI-Brookings Joint Center for Regulatory Studies, December 2001, available at http://www.aei-brookings.org/publications/related/oversight.pdf. For an early, insightful study on the importance of cost-benefit analysis in decision making, see John A. Hird, "Environmental Policy and Equity: The Case of Superfund," *Journal of Policy Analysis and Management* 12 (1993): 323.

94. See Cass Sunstein, *Risk and Reason*. See also Stephen Breyer, *Breaking the Vicious Circle*.

95. Parker makes charges against all three studies. See Parker, "Grading the Government," 1359: "This Part applies to regulatory scorecards the most basic test of scholarship: are the data reliable and the results

replicable? It will be seen that all three studies fail this basic test." See also Parker, "Grading the Government," 1375: "The Morrall and Hahn studies may use unreliable data and dubious methods, but at least their conclusions follow from their data. The same cannot be said of the Tengs/Graham studies."

96. For Heinzerling's critique of Morrall's table, see Heinzerling, "Mythic Proportions," 1981, stating, "[A] large percentage of the regulations appearing at the bottom of Morrall's list—the allegedly costliest regulations—have never taken effect. Many of these rules were rejected precisely because the agencies in question determined that their benefits did not justify their costs. Equally striking is the disparity between the agencies' (often implicit) estimates of costs per life saved and Morrall's estimates of such costs. Morrall's estimates are inevitably higher than the agencies' implicit estimates, sometimes as much as 1000 times higher." First, Heinzerling disagrees with Morrall's discounting of human lives. Second, she suggests that Morrall ignores many benefits of health and environmental regulation that are not susceptible to quantification and range beyond human health. Third, she believes that Morrall's table has selection bias, criticizing Morrall for including rules that were once proposed but never issued and excluding rules with benefits that far exceeded costs.

97. Parker suggests that Morrall alters agency estimates without acknowledging that he is doing so. See Parker, "Grading the Government," 1359, n.47: "Morrall also alters agency cost estimates without acknowledging that he is doing so. . . . Only by independent investigation did the author learn that Morrall substituted his new number of $1.3 billion per year for the agency estimate of $97 million per year." For Morrall's response to Parker's allegation, see "Saving Lives," 11, stating, "He [Parker] arrives at this conclusion, which is contrary to what is stated in the article, after a phone conversation. I said that I used a cost estimate of $1.3 billion annually for EPA's 1986 proposed Land Disposal regulation. Since he apparently assumed the agency estimate was $97 million based on the Heinzerling (1998) article. . . a careful independent investigation would have revealed that Heinzerling substituted a different regulatory proposal for the one in the table. The land disposal regulation in the table was published in the *Federal Register* on January 14, 1986. Its cost estimate was $1.3 billion annually (51 FR 1602). My independent investigation found that he substituted a different land disposal rule, one published in the *Federal Register* on December 11, 1986 that contained a $97 million cost estimate, for the one in the table."

98. Quantitatively oriented scholars seem to have created a burgeoning cottage industry for the critics and their colleagues. I suspect the critics and

those more supportive of economic analysis of regulation will keep each other fully employed for the foreseeable future. See Lisa Heinzerling and Frank Ackerman, "The Humbugs of the Anti-Regulatory Movement," *Cornell Law Review* 87 (2002): 648 (hereinafter "Humbugs"), stating, "Modern regulatory critics' style of argument bears an uncanny resemblance to these modes of argument which other reactionary movements have historically found useful. That the critics' general mode of argument follows a well-worn path might explain why the empirical details of their argument have escaped critical scrutiny. Indeed, the statistics drawn from the studies discussed in this Comment have been cited uncritically in everything from law review articles to congressional testimony to newspaper opinion pieces. No one seems to have considered the possibility that these numbers might be wrong, and wrong by a wide margin."

99. See Thomas O. McGarity, *Reinventing Rationality*, 153, stating, "Unfortunately many RIAs do not address distributional considerations. Even when distributional impacts are factored into an analysis, they tend to be treated as 'side constraints,' rather than as policy goals worthy of respect in their own right. One reason for this ambivalence toward distributional concerns may be the relative immunity of distributional considerations to quantitative analysis." Economic analyses could address distributional issues, but integrating distributional issues into cost-benefit analyses is hard.

100. Cost-benefit analysis could address such equity issues by adjusting utility weights for different groups. One can apply concepts of expected utility using weighted averages to equity issues. For an explanation of expected utility, see Michael Parkin, *Economics*, 3d ed. (Boston: Addison-Wesley Publishing, 1995), stating, "When there is uncertainty, people do not know the *actual* utility they will get from taking a particular course of action. But it is possible to calculate the utility they *expect* to get. Expected utility is the average utility arising from all possible outcomes. . . . Suppose [Tania] takes the telemarketing job. If she makes $9,000, her utility is 95 units, and if she makes $3,000, her utility is 65 units. Tania's *expected income* is the average of these two outcomes and is $6,000—($9,000 * .5) + ($3,000 * .5). This average is called a *weighted average*, the weights being the probabilities of each outcome (both .5 in this case). Tania's expected utility is the average of these two possible total utilities and is 80 units—(95 * .5) + (65 * .5)." Similarly, if the expected benefits from a regulation are three times as high for the poorer half of the population as for the richer half, then one could take a weighted average of the benefits for each group to calculate the total benefits. One could also extrapolate the benefits to each group if total benefits and weights for each group are known.

101. See Sheila Cavanaugh, Robert Hahn, and Robert Stavins, "Environmental Regulation During the 1990's: A Retrospective Analysis," *Harvard Environmental Law Review* 27, no. 2 (2003), available at http://www.aei-brookings.org/publications/abstract.php?pid=152, stating, "During the 1990s, the regulatory review process acquired a new focus on distributional concerns. In addition to requiring RIAs, Clinton's EO 12866 instructs agencies to select regulatory approaches that maximize net benefits, *including distributive impacts and equity*, unless a statute requires another regulatory approach. The language of the EO implicitly includes equity in the objective function to be maximized, although it is not clear how equity should or can be 'maximized.' In practice, agencies have responded to the order by including a separate distributional impact analysis within RIAs." Although agencies include a separate distributional impact analysis within some of their RIAs, they do not obtain adequate information on these impacts.

102. Distributional concerns are not considered to the extent we would like in regulatory impact analyses.

103. An exception may be gasoline taxes, which have been studied in some detail but on which there is considerable disagreement. See James M. Poterba, "Is the Gasoline Tax Regressive?" in *Tax Policy and the Economy*, ed. David Bradford, 145–64 (Cambridge, Mass.: The MIT Press, 1991).

104. Income redistribution does not necessarily work well when consumers do not view commodities as substitutable. For an instructive discussion of equity issues and risk regulation, see Cass Sunstein, *Risk and Reason*, 74–76, stating: "[R]egulators should be permitted to give *distributional weights* to risks whose distributional incidence is especially troublesome. . . . Most importantly, risk regulation may not be an effective way to pursue distributional justice. . . . As a general rule, redistribution through regulation is a notoriously unreliable way to help the most disadvantaged; a high minimum wage, for example, does not transfer resources directly from 'employers' to 'employees.' The costs of a high minimum wage are borne partly by consumers, who will pay higher prices, and partly by people who are frozen out of the job market. . . . But we are now dealing with regulation accompanied by distributional weights, and there is some hope for success here." See also Arrow et al., "Benefit-Cost Principles," 8: "Usually it is better to address concerns about local spillover effects of regulation by using tax and transfer policies rather than regulatory policy."

105. See E. J. Mishan, *Cost-Benefit Analysis* (New York: Praeger, 1976), discussing regulation and distributional effects.

106. See Hahn, Government Numbers II, 38, cited in note 24, for a discussion of how Hahn used the government's numbers: "I used the

government's numbers provided in the regulatory impact analyses to aggregate the benefits and costs of regulations from 1981 to mid-1996, to determine which regulations pass a cost-benefit test, and to identify factors that explain the variation in the estimates of regulatory cost-effectiveness. My analysis of the RIAs took agency estimates of the impact of regulations on the economy as given."

107. See Hahn, Government Numbers I, 211, cited in note 25, for a review of the literature and methodology used in my earlier study. This study examines RIAs in the period from 1990 to 1996. The part of the analysis that includes data before 1990 focuses primarily on cost-effectiveness. See Hahn, Government Numbers II, 384, n. 3, cited in note 24, for an introduction to the later study, or *the study*. The study is based on a review of all rules with regulatory impact analyses, or RIAs, that I could locate from 1981 through mid-1996, a total of 168 final and proposed rules. "The study builds on my earlier work, a study of ninety-two environmental, health, and safety regulations from 1990 to mid-1996, and is part of a continuing project to track the costs and benefits of federal regulation. I added seventy-six regulations to the original database, some from 1981 to 1990 and some from 1995 to 1996."

108. See Hahn, Government Numbers II, 84, n. 4, cited in note 24, for definitions of *RIA* and *major* regulations.

109. See Hahn, Government Numbers II, 33: "I discuss the extent to which federal agencies have catalogued information on the benefits and costs of regulatory activities, the role of benefit-cost analysis in the regulatory process, factors affecting the efficiency of regulation, and the relationship between a statute's requirements for economic analysis and the net benefits of regulations from that statute. . . . After assessing the quality of various agencies' estimates of the benefits and costs of regulation, I present the key analytical results concerning the net benefits of federal regulations for which an agency provided enough information to calculate net benefits. I also estimate the cost-effectiveness of selected regulations." My interest in examining the government's numbers was straightforward. Up to that point, no one had looked at microdata analyzing a large range of government regulations. I wanted to take a systematic look at the data to assess the quality and see what general conclusions I might draw about the impacts of regulation. I had no strong preconceptions regarding the benefit and cost data.

110. I use the words *the study* to refer to the second, more recent study on the costs and benefits of regulation that relies on the government's numbers.

111. For a more detailed discussion of the choice of discount rate, see section II, note 47; for a more detailed discussion of the value of a

statistical life, see the discussion in section III, pages 24–25, "Value of Life Is Too Low." See also Hahn, Government Numbers I and Government Numbers II for a discussion of discount rate and the value of statistical life. For a good definition and illustration of the value of a statistical life, see Viscusi, *Fatal Tradeoffs*, chapter 2.2, "The Value of Statistical Lives": "Suppose that our municipality could relocate its landfill to decrease fatality risk from our drinking water by 1/100,000. Suppose that you were willing to pay $20 for a risk reduction of this magnitude. . . . Suppose that there are 100,000 people at risk. On average, one expected life will be saved by the relocation of the landfill. As a group, the 100,000 residents are willing to pay $2 million ($20 * 100,000) for the one expected life saved. The economic value of this one expected life saved is consequently $2 million. This result is frequently termed the 'value of life,' even though this terminology implies in a somewhat misleading manner that what we are valuing is certain lives rather than statistical lives involving very small probabilities. Another way of conceptualizing this calculation is to view it as simply ascertaining the value we are willing to pay per unit risk. Viewed in this manner, one estimates the value of a statistical life by dividing our willingness to pay for added safety ($2) by the risk increment that is involved (1/100,000), with the result being the same—$2 million. It is important to recognize what these tradeoffs mean. They only reflect attitudes toward small probabilities. They do not imply that we would accept certain death in return for $2 million, or even that we would accept a .5 probability of death for $1 million."

112. See Parker, "Grading the Government," 1361: "For example, he excludes cost savings from regulations because he believes those savings are generally questionable."

113. See Hahn, Government Numbers I, 229: "Nonetheless, I shall also consider the case in which the analysis includes those cost savings." See also Government Numbers II, 86, n. 16, revealing that Hahn includes cost savings in the analysis: "I combine cost savings and benefits in this analysis, although economists generally believe that most estimates of cost savings are implausible."

114. See the discussion of sensitivity analyses in section III. An interesting question for future research might be the extent to which analyses, in particular RIAs, deviate from the standards at the time. This, however, was not the focus of my research.

115. See Parker, "Grading the Government," 30. Parker states, "Hahn's 2000 study does not even account for *inflation* after 1990." See also Parker, "Grading the Government," 30, n. 109: "[U]sing the same $3–7 million range that Viscusi puts forward in 1992, in 1990 dollars, for benefits

expressed in 1995 dollars. Simply accounting for inflation over that five year period would raise the base case life value from $5 million to $6 million."

116. See the discussion in Hahn, Government Numbers II, 39: "To make the analysis consistent across different programs and regulations and to allow for aggregation of net benefits, I converted all dollar estimates to the same dollar base year. In that way I corrected for inflation and further discounted all dollar estimates to reflect the social opportunity cost of investing the regulation. I first used the consumer price index to convert all annualized estimates of costs and benefits for each regulation to 1995 dollars."

117. In general, if prices increase over time and net benefits are positive, choosing an earlier year results in a smaller value for net benefits.

118. Parker highlights the fact that my choice of a base year to discount cost and benefits is "arbitrary." See Parker, "Grading the Government," 1361: "Costs and benefits that occur before or after 1996 are discounted forward or back to that arbitrary base year—a practice unique to Hahn which (Hahn admits) has a major effect on numerical outcomes." I run a sensitivity analysis on my results to illustrate the effects of changing the base year, but Parker seems to be focused on the fact that my choice of year is arbitrary. Moreover, adjustments to the base year do not affect the number of regulations that pass a cost-benefit test.

119. See Portney and Weyant, *Discounting and Intergenerational Equity*, cited in note 45, for a discussion of the need to discount future benefits and costs at some positive rate.

120. See Hahn, Government Numbers II, 39, cited in note 116, discussing the reasons for converting all dollar estimates to the same base year.

121. See Hahn, Government Numbers II, 45: "Varying the base year for the present-value calculation significantly affects the magnitude of the estimates. It was necessary to choose a base year to standardize the data, but the choice was difficult because the benefits and costs of regulations accrue over different periods of time from 1981 onward and therefore have different base years. The choice of an earlier base year than 1996, the year I chose for the analysis, lowers the net benefits of regulations because the value of benefits in the future decreases for regulations promulgated later. . . . Similarly, using 2010 as the base year would nearly double the present-value estimate. That analysis suggests that we need to treat the aggregate benefit numbers with great care because no obvious choice for a base year exists. I chose 1996 for the base year because that was the 'present' for my analysis." See also Hahn, Government Numbers II, 47, figure 3-2, for net benefits as a function of the discount rate for base years 1980, 1996, and 2010.

122. See Parker, "Grading the Government," 1409. Parker states, "One of the most striking features of the Hahn, Morrall and Graham/Tengs score-cards—and, one suspects, a key to their great influence—is the precision of their numbers, which they typically report to three or four significant digits. Yet the appearance of precision is highly misleading."

123. See Parker, "Grading the Government," 1361: "In the many cases in which agencies indicate a range of costs or benefits, Hahn collapses the range and takes only the mid-point, even where the agency has specified a different point in the range as more plausible." Contrary to Parker's statement, agencies infrequently provide ranges in their regulatory impact analyses. In cases where the agencies provided a range, we used the midpoint of the range. For a discussion of ranges and best estimates in agency RIAs, see Hahn et al., "Assessing Regulatory Impact Analyses," 867. We provide sensitivity analyses to account for uncertainty in this section.

124. Two significant digits are probably reasonable but certainly not four.

125. See Parker, "Grading the Government," 1369: "Predictions which ignore dynamic policy adaptation will tend to understate the net benefits of regulation. To take just one example, EPA's Final Great Lakes Water Quality Guidance aims to curtail emissions of persistent, bio-accumulative toxic pollutants into the Great Lakes. EPA anticipated an annualized compliance cost of between $60 and $380 million per year ($1994). But EPA also said that it expected costs to be near the low end of the range. . . . Yet Hahn's scorecard ignores this corrective mechanism. It mechanically adopts the mid-point estimate of $218 million."

126. See Hahn et al., "Assessing Regulatory Impact Analyses," 868, figure 2: "Only 17 percent of the rules presented both a best estimate and a range of those quantitative benefits."

127. See Hahn et al., "Assessing Regulatory Impact Analyses," 867: "Figure 1 also shows that agencies presented a 'best estimate' of monetized costs far more often than they presented an actual range. Over two-thirds of the regulations gave a best estimate of costs, while only one-fourth presented a range of cost estimates."

128. See Final water quality guidance for the Great Lakes system, *Federal Register* 60 (March 23, 1995): 15,381.

129. See Final water quality guidance for the Great Lakes system, *Federal Register* 60 (March 23, 1995): 15,381, for a description of these opportunity costs: "In addition to the cost estimates described above, EPA estimated the cost to comply with requirements consistent with the antidegradation provisions of the final Guidance. This potential future cost is expressed as a 'lost opportunity' cost for facilities impacted by the

antidegradation requirements. This cost could result in the addition of about $22 million each year."

130. In effect, ranges are introduced through the use of sensitivity analyses on a number of key variables. Moreover, agencies appear to offer ranges in RIAs infrequently and they do not always provide a rationale for the ranges. Subsequent research motivated in part by the study makes clear that there is a problem with the presentation of ranges. Even if I had used both the ranges and best estimates given, this issue would not have been totally resolved. RIAs rarely express exactly what their range represents (i.e., an $x\%$ confidence interval). Nor are all ranges necessarily standardized. One may be a range of feasible values, another a range of likely values, and a third simply a range of possible values. While agencies often discuss issues of uncertainty, they describe that uncertainty in quantitative terms less often. A meaningful sensitivity analysis on all factors related to each rule, as Parker suggests, would have been a massive undertaking.

131. See Robert W. Hahn, Randall Lutter, and W. Kip Viscusi, *Do Federal Regulations Reduce Mortality?* (Washington, D.C.: AEI-Brookings Joint Center for Regulatory Studies, 2000) (hereinafter Hahn, Lutter, and Viscusi).

132. See Viscusi, "Fatal Tradeoffs," cited in note 19, for a definition of VSL.

133. The base case includes all 106 final rules and uses a VSL of $5 million ($1994) and a discount rate of 5 percent.

134. I also did not count narrations of costs in tallying up monetary benefits and costs. I present some sensitivity analyses later on benefits and costs that address the potential importance of this issue.

135. See Parker, "Grading the Government," 1382: "Perusing Hahn's unpublished spreadsheet of regulatory costs and benefits (reproduced in Annex C) yields a startling discovery. Forty-one of the 136 rules in his database—fully thirty percent of all the rules—are assigned a zero benefit."

136. See section II, table 1 for the regulatory scorecard.

137. See Hahn, Government Numbers II, 35: "For 98 percent of the cases, agencies reported information on costs. Agencies assessed benefits, cost savings, or both for 87 percent of the rules." Benefits were monetized for only 26 percent of the rules. Multiple passages in the text warn readers that the information from the RIAs is incomplete. See also Hahn, Government Numbers II, 34: "Scholars have found that the information provided in the RIA is often not complete and that the level of detail and analytical sophistication varies across agencies and types of regulations. Common deficiencies cited throughout much of the literature include inadequate consideration of alternatives, poor treatment of uncertainty, incomplete estimation of benefits and costs, and various methodological errors. . . . Perhaps most

important, in many cases a particular agency did not complete its quantitative analysis of benefits or cost savings." Moreover, I referred the reader to three studies conducted by the General Accounting Office that backed up these conclusions. See, e.g., Hahn, Government Numbers II, 86, n. 15: "The General Accounting Office (1997, 1998, 1999) has conducted three additional studies that support those conclusions." Other research I conducted elaborates on these issues. Nonetheless, in retrospect, it may have been useful to explicitly state that I was not able to completely overcome the deficiencies of my data source.

138. We monetized many of the benefits that the agency quantified but did not monetize for the ninety-seven regulations. See Robert Hahn, Rohit Malik, and Patrick Dudley, *Reviewing the Government's Numbers on Regulation* (2004), available at www.aei-brookings.org (hereinafter *Reviewing Government's Numbers*) for benefits by each regulation.

139. See Parker, "Grading the Government," 1381, discussing Hahn's assignment of zero benefits to regulations: "This Part discusses three such shortcomings: (A) The disregard of whole categories of unquantified costs and benefits (and, amazingly, many benefits that the agencies quantified). . . . It turns out that Hahn, with a few narrow and limited exceptions, has assigned a zero value to any benefit which the government's regulatory impact assessment does not quantify and monetize. . . . All unquantifed benefits are assigned a zero value. As seen in more detail below, Hahn will monetize the value of a benefit which the agency has quantified but not monetized in the case of benefits involving (1) avoidance of cancer, heart disease or lead poisoning, (2) avoiding of accidental death or injury; and (3) pollution from any of four named air pollutants." See also Shapiro and Glicksman, *Pragmatic Balance*, 77: "Hahn supplied his own estimate of the value of the benefits when agencies failed to monetize the value of the lives that a regulation was projected to save. This adjustment also decreased his net benefit estimate."

140. See section II, table 1.

141. See Hahn, Government Numbers II, 57–59, tables 3-9 and 3-10: "I found that agencies stated that a rule passes a cost-benefit test for 23 percent of all rules—39 of 168. Agencies did not monetize benefits for many of those rules, however. Nine rules pass a cost-benefit test without monetizing benefits because of net cost savings. Of the rules for which the agency monetized benefits, 75 percent—thirty of forty-four—pass a cost-benefit test. . . . Table 3-10 shows how the number of rules passing a cost-benefit test varies with assumptions about the discount rate and valuation of benefits. The number of rules that pass a benefit-cost test is most dependent on

the value of benefits. . . . Changes in the value of a unit of air pollution reduction have a marked effect on the net benefits of Clean Air Act rules."

142. See the discussion in section IV.

143. See Hahn, Government Numbers II, 38–40: "As is clear from the previous section, the government's numbers are often the result of incomplete—and sometimes even flawed—analysis. . . . All agencies, including the EPA, did not often provide quantified estimates of environmental benefits other than air pollution reduction benefits. My analysis therefore includes only air pollution reduction benefits. To calculate the total benefits of a rule, I combined the benefits from health and safety risk reduction with the benefits from air pollution reduction."

144. For example, it is easy to claim that some unquantified ecosystem benefits are associated with every environmental regulation as well as unquantified indirect costs on management, innovation, and the states. It is not always immediately apparent how to treat such information. In a similar vein, the requirement to discuss environmental equity impacts of regulation has not yielded much useful information on that subject. See, e.g., Robert Hahn, Sheila Olmstead, and Robert Stavins, "Environmental Regulation during the 1990s: A Retrospective Analysis," *Harvard Environmental Law Review* 27, no. 2 (2003): 377–415 for a discussion of environmental equity.

145. See Parker, "Grading the Government," 1380, n. 134: "All unquantified benefits are assigned a zero value." Maybe that assumption is unreasonable, but I am unaware of an alternative. Parker does not offer an alternative proposal for treating unquantified benefits, other than to abandon scorecards altogether. Parker describes this issue as one of "a number of analytical defects endemic to the scorecard enterprise." See Parker, "Grading the Government," 1381.

146. If one were doing a more in-depth study of particular regulations, it might be possible to obtain some quantifiable estimates using expert judgment or some other method. But this is precisely what the agencies should be doing. See, e.g., Kenneth J. Arrow et al., *Benefit-Cost Principles.*

147. See Robert W. Hahn and Rohit Malik, "Is Regulation Good For You?" *Harvard Journal of Law and Public Policy* 27, no. 3 (2004): 893–916, available at http://www.aei-brookings.com/publications/abstract.php?pid=757.

148. See Hahn, Government Numbers II, 35, 38, for an elaboration of the difficulties in quantifying benefits for process-oriented rules: "Many of the rules lacking benefit estimates are process-oriented, such as rules that require third parties to gather information or outline the structure of

government programs. The benefits of process-oriented rules are often difficult to identify, much less to quantify." Parker argues that scorecards (by his definition of scorecard) are not equipped to deal with them since they assign zero benefits to these rules. See Parker, "Grading the Government," 1405: "The culpability of scorecards is found, not in their failure to detect previously unidentified costs and benefits, but in their omission of costs and benefits which agencies identify and describe narratively, but do not pretend to be able to quantify or monetize. These are omissions that violate cardinal principles of cost-benefit analysis, that are unique to scorecards, and that call the viability of scorecards into serious question."

149. See Hahn, Government Numbers I, 40, table 10-3, Key Parameters of the Model: "Note: All dollar figures have been adjusted to 1994 dollars using implicit price deflators." For the most updated study and assumptions for year dollars, see Hahn, Government Numbers II, 40, table 3-3, Key Parameters of the Model: "Note: I adjusted all dollar figures to 1994 dollars by using implicit price deflators (Council of Economic Advisers 1995). I updated those figures to 1995 dollars in the rest of this chapter."

150. These experts included Al McGartland and W. Kip Viscusi.

151. See Parker, "Grading the Government," 1370: "Hahn, as we have seen, assigns a 'standard' value of $5 million per statistical life saved, with $3 million and $7 million values used in sensitivity analysis. . . . Such practices are now commonplace in agency analysis as well. . . . This section simply argues, building on the work of Revesz and others, that the risk-to-life-values in current use are not empirically well-grounded, and are far too low by their own interior logic."

152. See Science Advisory Board 812 Report, Letter to Carol Browner, 6: "We also believe that the value currently applied to a statistical life, $4.8 million (1990 U.S. dollars) significantly overstates the value most people would attach to the average number of life years saved (per person) by the CAA. If the $4.8 million (1990 U.S. dollars) figure is retained, it should be made clear that this was derived as the value of saving the statistical life of a 40-year old."

153. See W. Kip Viscusi and Joseph E. Aldy, "The Value of a Statistical Life: A Critical Review of Market Estimates Throughout the World," NBER Working Paper No. 9487 (February 2003), 26: "Our median estimated VSL from Table 2 is about $7 million, which is in line with the estimates from the studies that we regard as most reliable." This article reviews more than sixty studies of mortality risk premiums from ten countries and approximately forty studies that present estimates of injury risk premiums in total

from ten countries but does not include contingent valuation (CV) studies. Introducing CV studies would reduce that value because these have resulted in lower values. See, e.g., Anna Alberini, Maureen Cropper, Alan Krupnick, and Nathalie Simon, "Does the Value of a Statistical Life Vary with Age and Health Status? Evidence from the United States and Canada," *Resources for the Future* (April 2002), available at http://www.rff.org/disc_papers/PDF_files/0219.pdf, showing that the willingness to pay for mortality risk reductions does not decline with age in the United States.

154. See Parker, "Grading the Government," 31: "What is the net effect of the omitted adjustments on Hahn's assumed life values? As Annex E indicates, the net effect may well be an understatement of the value of life by a factor of 3.5–5.5."

155. See Parker, "Grading the Government," 1485–86, appendix D, illustrating the effects of growth in real income on the value of life. See also Parker, "Grading the Government," 28, for a discussion of the effects of involuntary risks on the value of life: "Most scholars agree that involuntary risks should be valued more highly than voluntary ones: some say twice as high."

156. See Parker, "Grading the Government," 31: "One response to the problems of valuation identified above is, obviously, to recommend raising the estimated value of life to reflect the required adjustments. . . . Another, more candid, response, in this author's view, would be simply to conclude that both the primary values and the adjustments are too speculative to warrant much reliance: we simply do not *know* what the income elasticity of risk value is, or how to adjust for involuntary, cumulative, or dread risks." A better response is to account for uncertainties in valuation of life by doing sensitivity analyses. See Hahn, Government Numbers I, Government Numbers II, and section III in the present work for sensitivity analyses.

157. See U.S. Environmental Protection Agency, "Valuing the Benefits of Fatal Cancer Risk Reduction," SAB Report on the EPA's White Paper, EPA-SAB-EEAC-00-013 (Washington, D.C.: Environmental Protection Agency, 1999) (hereinafter SAB Report) for a rejection of Revesz's adjustments to the VSL: "The Committee disagrees with Revesz' suggestion that VSL for an immediate fatality be adjusted by 'at least a factor of two' to capture morbidity, fear, and dread associated with cancer. Revesz also cites a study by Cropper and Subramanian (1999) to justify multiplying VSL by a factor of two for risks that are involuntary and difficult to control. The Committee does not believe that any such adjustment is warranted by the Cropper and Subramanian study. . . . The EEAC does not agree with the suggestion that

the VSL be adjusted upward because workers in labor market studies earn less, on average, than median earnings of all U.S. workers (Revesz 1999), because of the sensitivity of making such distinctions, and because of insufficient evidence available at present." See also U.S. Environmental Protection Agency, "Review of the Draft Analytical Plan for EPA's Second Prospective Analysis—Benefits and Costs of the Clean Air Act 1990–2020: An Advisory by a Special Panel of the Advisory Council on Clean Air Compliance Analysis," EPA-SAB-Council-ADV-04-004 (Washington, D.C.: Environmental Protection Agency September 2001), 23–25, for a discussion of potential adjustments to the value of statistical life: "[N]o adjustment is made for differences in income, baseline risk, or other factors that may influence VSL (for example, the inflation adjustment makes implicit assumptions about the income elasticity and growth of income relative to cost-of-living. . . . With regard to adjusting for income growth, EPA proposes to value future changes in mortality risk using a VSL that increases to account for anticipated increases in real income. This approach is conceptually appropriate, but there is substantial uncertainty about the appropriate income elasticity to use. . . . Ideally, it would help to control explicitly for age in all VSL studies. However, many studies do not consider the VSL for a wide-enough age spectrum to isolate the impact of age. Thus, at present, it seems necessary to use VSL estimates from one age group to approximate the VSL of another group, although meta-analytical techniques hold some promise for identifying the likely effects of age on estimated VSLs. . . . The relatively clear logic for adjusting VSLs for assumed increases in average real income over time might seem to suggest that VSLs should also be adjusted for current and future cross-sectional differences in individual incomes. However, such adjustments do not appear to be practical, since they would require very disaggregated modeling of changes in air quality and human exposure to air pollution. Moreover, the Council suspects that adjustments for income would have little effect on estimated benefits, because effects of fine particles, ozone, and other major pollutants are distributed across broad geographic areas which contain wide variations in income." The SAB does not discuss voluntary vs. involuntary risks. The SAB seems to think that the adjustments are correct in theory, but impractical.

158. This range compares to a range of 35–45 percent, with a base case value of 43 percent, when zero benefits are included. The set of regulations with zero benefits could include process regulations as well as nonprocess regulations. For example, some process regulations that are removed from this reduced data set include Fuels and Fuel Additives Registration Requirements as well as the Operating Permits Regulation Under Title V of

the Clean Air Act. However, other nonprocess regulations, such as the Mechanical Power Press Standard and a Clean Water Act regulation concerning Electroplating and Metal Finishing, are also removed. Of the forty-one rules that Parker identifies as having zero benefits, eleven had cost savings that were counted in the model.

159. See Parker, "Grading the Government," 1384: "Hahn likewise excludes benefits which agencies have quantified and monetized, but which do not fit into one of his arbitrary categories—even as he insists that he is using the 'government's numbers'." This criticism is correct and was an oversight. I ran a sensitivity analysis on this but neglected to report it. I report it in this section. There are two nonstandard issues: one is the nonstandard, monetized benefits we cover in our sensitivity analysis; the other includes benefits that the agency quantified but did not monetize and that we did not monetize because we did not know how. The Agricultural Worker Protection rule is an example of the latter.

160. See table 6. In almost all cases, there is a 2 percent increase in the number of regulations that would pass a cost-benefit test. The only exception occurs in the unlikely scenario that an additional 3 percent of regulations would pass (where the VSL is $1 million, and the discount rate is 9 percent).

161. The only exception occurs in the unlikely scenario that an additional 3 percent of regulations would pass (where the VSL is $1 million, and the discount rate is 9 percent).

162. See Parker, "Grading the Government," 1383: "The omissions of unquantified variables are not confined to zero-benefit rules. Rules that display a positive number in the benefits column turn out, on closer inspection, to have had whole categories of important benefits excluded from the tally. The result is forty-one zero-benefit rules and an indeterminate number of other rules for which whole categories of benefits have been summarily excluded."

163. See Hahn, Lutter, and Viscusi, *Do Federal Regulations Reduce Mortality?* 15: "Those regulations are the most logical candidates for our analysis because their primary effect is to reduce mortality risk." This is subjective, because the full benefits cannot be known. We made this determination by examining the intent of the rule and the listed benefits. The regulations in this sample include several regulations from Government Numbers I, and some additional regulations. See Hahn, Lutter, and Viscusi, 14–15 for details: "We begin with a database of essentially all final regulations issued by federal agencies to reduce environmental, health, or safety risks between 1991 and June 1998. Hahn previously compiled a database

that included all regulations between 1991 and the middle of 1996 and classified as major or economically significant under the two executive orders addressing regulatory review, Executive Order 12291 and Executive Order 12866. To that set we added rules from the middle of 1996 until 1998 that were analyzed as part of the AEI-Brookings Joint Center Regulatory Improvement Project. We limit our analysis to those regulations that we estimate had mortality benefits that were at least 90 percent of total benefits, according to agency estimates."

164. Of course the sample is different. For more sensitivity analyses using varying income-mortality cutoffs, see Hahn, Lutter, and Viscusi, 21, figure 3-2, Rules Failing an Income-Mortality or Benefit-Cost Test.

165. For example, the range for the percent of rules passing a cost-benefit test expands by only 1 percent for all regulations from 36–45 percent when the VSL varies from $3 million to $7 million, and the discount rate varies from 3–7 percent to 35–45 percent when the VSL varies from $1 million to $9 million and the discount rate varies from 1 percent to 9 percent.

166. The best-case scenarios are those for which the percentage of rules passing a cost-benefit test is high. The best cases occur when we assume a high VSL, between $7 million and $9 million.

167. See Parker, "Grading the Government," 1400–1402; "The score-cardists' omission of unquantified variables is not confined to the benefits column. Economists have long recognized that government regulations bring with them an array of indirect costs and cost savings that tend to be overlooked to varying degrees in agency RIAs and scorecards alike. . . . Nonetheless, the scorecardists' omission of unquantified costs in scorecards is more understandable than their treatment of benefits in one respect: agencies do not normally offer a narrative description of the various costs that are being overlooked in particular cases." See also McGarity, *Reinventing Rationality*, 127–28, describing difficulties that agencies face in deriving reliable cost estimates.

168. For a more in-depth discussion of agency exclusion of some costs, see Hahn and Hird, "Costs and Benefits," cited in note 41.

169. Parker correctly notes that agencies do not account for costs associated with "ancillary risks" that result from risk-reducing regulations, but this is well known. See Parker, "Grading the Government," 1404: "Whatever the reason, risk-risk tradeoffs are typically slighted in agency assessments and scorecards alike. These tradeoffs count as unquantified 'costs' of regulation, the omission of which tends to over-state the net benefits of regulation." For a good analysis of such risk-risk tradeoffs, see Randall Lutter and Christopher Wolz, "UV-B Screening by Tropospheric Ozone: Implications

for the National Ambient Air Quality Standard," *Environmental Science and Technology* 31 (1997): 142A–146A. For an argument suggesting the need for the EPA to employ such risk-risk tradeoffs, see Randall Lutter and Howard Gruenspecht, "Assessing Benefits of Ground-Level Ozone: What Role for Science in Setting National Air Quality Standards?" AEI-Brookings Joint Center for Regulatory Studies, available at http://aei-brookings.org/admin/pdffiles/reg_analysis_01_04.pdf. For excellent treatments of risk-risk analysis, see also Lester Lave, *The Strategy of Social Regulation: Decision Frameworks for Policy* (Washington, D.C.: Brookings Institution Press, 1981). For a discussion of risk-risk tradeoffs, see Sunstein, *Risk and Reason*, cited in note 4. See also John Graham and Jonathan Wiener, *Risk vs. Risk, Tradeoffs in Protecting Health and the Environment* (Cambridge, Mass.: Harvard University Press, 1995). See Richard Revesz, "Environmental Regulation, Cost-Benefit Analysis, and the Discounting of Human Lives," *Columbia Law Review* 99 (1999): 941 (hereinafter "Environmental Regulation and Discounting of Human Lives"), for an elegant generalization of this idea.

170. See Michael Hazilla and Raymond Kopp, "Social Cost of Environmental Quality Regulations: A General Equilibrium Analysis," *Journal of Political Economics* 98 (1990): 853, for the importance of taking economywide effects into account (finding that second-order effects are pronounced in air and water regulation and social costs increased above the EPA's estimate of compliance costs in the 1980s).

171. See Heinzerling and Ackerman, "Humbugs," 648: "The numbers served up by these studies cannot help but perplex and disturb you, even if (maybe especially if) you are in favor of protecting human health and the environment." See also Parker, "Grading the Government," 1353, referring to scorecards as the "empirical foundation for the anti-regulatory fervor that has gripped Congress, academia and millions of Americans for over a decade." Parker also states that Hahn and Morrall have an antiregulatory bias. See also Parker, "Grading the Government," 1364: "Moreover, his [Morrall's] focus on proposed or enacted rules (as opposed to regulatory opportunities) introduces a further anti-regulatory bias, as will be seen in the following discussion of Hahn's scorecard. . . . Hahn, however, follows OMB in defining 'minor rules' as those that cost more than $100 million per year to comply with. . . . The result is an in-built sampling bias against regulation."

172. The problem is quite complex. See Harrington et al., "Regulatory Cost Estimates," cited in note 76, suggesting that agencies tend to overestimate costs and benefits in their regulatory analyses. Care must be taken in interpreting the frame of reference used by these authors and others who work

in this area. It is critical to know what costs and benefits are counted. See also Si Kyung Seong and John Mendeloff, *Assessing the Accuracy of OSHA's Projections of the Benefits of New Safety Standards*, cited in note 67, finding that OSHA appeared to overestimate the number of deaths prevented by six safety standards issued since 1990.

173. See Parker, "Grading the Government," 1361: "For example, he excludes cost savings from regulations because he believes 'those savings are generally questionable.'"

174. See Hahn, Government Numbers II, 86 n. 16: "I combine cost savings and benefits in this analysis, although economists generally believe that most estimates of cost savings are implausible. . . . In my database, for example, including cost savings leads to ten regulations that save money."

175. For a good explanation of problems with double counting in the context of energy efficiency, see Paul Joskow and Donald Marron, "What Does a Negawatt Really Cost: Evidence from Utility Conservation Programs," *Energy Journal* 13, no. 4 (December 1991): 47.

176. A good example of a regulation in which cost savings are double counted is the Control of Hazardous Energy Regulation, in which cost savings are $123 million annually.

177. See W. Kip Viscusi, "The Dangers of Unbounded Commitments to Regulate Risk," in *Risks, Costs and Lives Saved*, ed. Robert Hahn (New York: Oxford University Press, 1996), 162, offering the following two conclusions: "First, the cost-effectiveness of risk-regulation policies differs greatly across government agencies. We could clearly save more lives for less money through a reallocation of regulatory resources. Second, the trade-offs that are made are out of line with reasonable efforts to reduce risk. The cost per life saved amounts are inconsistent with measures of society's willingness to pay to save the lives." Viscusi and others could not have developed these insights without the information that scorecards have provided on the cost per life saved for a wide range of policy interventions.

178. See John Morrall, "Review of the Record," 31, table 4: "The most obvious implication of these figures is that the range of cost-effectiveness among rules is enormous. . . . Even excluding all proposed rules and the least cost-effective final rule, issued by the FDA, the range is still three orders of magnitude."

179. See Hahn, Government Numbers II, 48, figure 3-3, "Cost-Effectiveness of Selected Final Environmental, Health, and Safety Regulations," showing that cost-effectiveness varies over time and by agency.

180. See Morrall, "Saving Lives." See also Randall Lutter and John F. Morrall, "Health-Health Analysis," *Journal of Risk and Uncertainty* 8 (1994): 43.

181. See table 8. These results are millions of 1995 dollars, expressed as an annual total cost per discounted statistical life saved. Total costs include cost savings. Some sensitivity analyses are described in Hahn, Lutter, and Viscusi, 21. The fact that those regulations are aimed primarily at saving lives, based on the authors' assessment, addresses the critics' concern that cost-effectiveness may be misleading when other important benefits are not included in the measure of effectiveness.

182. Tengs et al., "Life-Saving Interventions," 373–84.

183. For a recent discussion, see Robert Stavins, *Experience with Market-Based Environmental Policy Instruments* (Washington, D.C.: Resources for the Future, 2003). See also A. Denny Ellerman et al., "Emissions Trading under the US Acid Rain Program: Evaluation of Compliance Costs and Allowance Market Performance" (Cambridge, Mass.: Center for Energy and Environmental Policy Research, Massachusetts Institute of Technology, 1997), for a discussion of the U.S. acid rain program, noting that "a rough estimate of the cost savings attributable to emissions trading in 1995 lies between $225 and $375 million, in current dollars, which implies that the cost of compliance with Title IV would have been one-third to one-half as costly had electric utilities simply reduced emissions without taking advantage of the emissions process."

184. For a discussion of some of these issues, see, e.g., Hahn and Stavins, "Economic Incentives." For a discussion of estimated cost savings, see Thomas H. Tietenberg, *Emissions Trading: An Exercise in Reforming Pollution Policy* (Washington, D.C.: Resources for the Future, 1985) (hereinafter *Emissions Trading*). See also Robert Hahn, "The Impact of Economics on Environmental Policy," *Journal of Environmental Economics and Management* 39, no. 3 (May 2000): 375 (hereinafter "Impact of Economics").

185. For a classic treatment, see J. H. Dales, *Pollution, Property, and Prices: An Essay in Policy-Making and Economics* (Toronto: University of Toronto, 1968).

186. Robert Crandall, *Controlling Industrial Pollution: The Economics and Politics of Clean Air* (Washington, D.C.: The Brookings Institution, June 1, 1983).

187. See Tengs et al., "Life-Saving Interventions," 371: "As summarized in Table I, while the median intervention described in the literature costs $42,000 per life-year saved (*n* = 587), the median medical intervention costs $19,000/life-year (*n* = 310); the median injury reduction intervention costs $48,000/life-year (*n* = 133); and the median toxin control intervention costs $2,800,000/life-year (*n* = 144)." See also R. H. Chapman et al., "A Comprehensive League Table of Cost-Utility Ratios and Sub-Table of

'Panel-Worthy' Studies," *Medical Decision-Making* 20, no. 4 (2000): 451–67. R. J. Zeckhauser and D. S. Shepard, "Where Now for Saving Lives? *Law and Contemporary Problems* 40, no. 4 (1976): 5–45.

188. For examples of "scorecards" in the public health literature, see Tengs et al., "Life-Saving Interventions," 373. See also P. J. Neumann et al., "Preference-Based Measures in Economic Evaluation in Health Care," *Annual Review of Public Health* 21 (2000): 587. See, e.g., J. Kupersmith, "Cost-Effectiveness Analysis in Heart Disease, Part I: General Principles," *Progress in Cardiovascular Diseases* 37, no. 3 (1994): 161.

189. See Morrall, "Review of the Record," 32–33: "[S]afety regulation appears to be far more cost-effective than health regulation. The median of cost-per-life-saved estimates for the cancer regulations . . . is 75 times higher than for the safety regulations—$37.6 million compared to $500,000. . . . [T]hese data suggest that regulatory reformers should attend not only to reducing the overregulation of cancer risks, but also to the possibility of increasing safety regulation."

190. See Morrall, "Saving Lives," table 2.

191. James T. Hamilton and W. Kip Viscusi, *Calculating Risks: The Spatial and Political Dimensions of Hazardous Waste Policy* (Cambridge, Mass.: The MIT Press, 1999), 127 (hereinafter *Calculating Risks*).

192. See, e.g., Morrall, "Review of the Record," 31: "In principle, the best measure of desirability is net social benefits; the value in dollars of the number of deaths averted by a regulation minus the cost of the regulation. Given a ranking of regulations by net social benefits, one would conclude that all those with positive net benefits are worthwhile policies and all those with negative net benefits are not (assuming, of course, one has confidence in the underlying data and the value-of-life figures)."

193. See the discussion in section III.

194. See A. Myrick Freeman, "Environmental Policy since Earth Day I: What Have We Gained?" *Journal of Economic Perspectives* 16, no. 1 (Winter 2002): 142 (hereinafter "Environmental Policy since Earth Day I"). Other winners include setting maximum allowable concentrations on some volatile organic compounds under the Safe Drinking Water Act and the cleanup of those hazardous waste sites with the lowest possible cost per cancer case avoided under Superfund.

195. See generally Freeman, "Environmental Policy since Earth Day I," 141–42, noting, "About 70 percent of the sites have estimated costs per case avoided that are greater than about $112 million, implying that unless there are significant benefits in such categories as avoiding noncancer health effects and ecological and natural resource effects, the majority of the

remediation plans are not economically justified." Other losers include mobile source air pollution control and much of the control of discharges into the nation's waterways, with the exception of some lakes and rivers that were especially polluted. See also Freeman, "Environmental Policy since Earth Day I," 138, noting that "the Clean Water Act does not appear to have achieved benefits commensurate with its costs." On policies aimed at controlling ozone, Freeman, 132, notes, "Even if all of the remaining $6 billion in benefits could be attributed to reductions in ozone concentrations due to Title II (and they cannot be), the total cost of Title II would be twice its benefits." See Freeman, 136: "If ozone does not cause premature mortality, then the proposed ozone standard does not appear to pass a cost-benefit test. . . . Thus, even the high-end positive net benefits are in doubt." See also James T. Hamilton and W. Kip Viscusi, "How Costly is 'Clean'? An Analysis of the Benefits and Costs of Superfund Remediations," *Journal of Policy Analysis and Management* 18, no. 1 (1999): 2. See also Hamilton and Viscusi, "Calculating Risks." See, e.g., Paul Portney, "Economics and the Clear Air Act," *Journal of Economic Perspectives* 4, no. 4 (1990): 173.

196. Such policies also include achieving a more socially desirable objective at the same or lower cost than some clearly specified alternative, such as the status quo.

197. See Hahn and Stavins, "Economic Incentives," cited in note 73, for a discussion of emissions trading.

198. See Tietenberg, "Emissions Trading"; Hahn, "Impact of Economics."

199. For more on factors affecting adoption, see, e.g., Robert W. Hahn and Roger G. Noll, "Environmental Markets in the Year 2000," *Journal of Risk and Uncertainty* 3, no. 4 (December 1990): 351. For some studies that review actual savings, see Stavins, *Experience with Market-Based Environmental Policy Instruments*, cited in note 183.

200. See Lutter and Morrall, "Health-Health Analysis," cited in note 180, for a discussion of health-health tradeoffs

201. For a listing of such policies in a scorecard, see Sunstein, *Risk and Reason*, 140, table 6.2. He borrows this table from Lutter and Morrall's table 1 in "Health-Health Analysis," stating, "The overall news is quite good: eleven regulations decrease mortality risks, and the savings from the beneficial regulations are far larger than the losses from the harmful regulations—so much so that as a whole, the regulations promise to save 6,400 lives each year."

202. See Sunstein, *Risk and Reason*, 139, table 6.1, for a scorecard that quantifies risk-risk or health-health tradeoffs.

203. See, e.g., Robert Hahn and Cass Sunstein, "A New Executive Order for Improving Federal Regulation? Deeper and Wider Cost-Benefit Analysis," *University of Pennsylvania Law Review* 150 (2002): 1489–1517. Hahn and Sunstein advocate that such substitution risks be considered in their proposed executive order for the OMB. See also Revesz, "Environmental Regulation and Discounting of Human Lives." Revesz describes situations in which the risk-risk test should be broadened to include ancillary benefits as well as risks.

204. See, e.g., Ralph L. Keeney, "Estimating Fatalities Induced by the Economic Costs of Regulations," *Journal of Risk and Uncertainty* 14, no. 1 (1990): 5, 24.

205. Ibid.

206. See Hahn, Lutter, and Viscusi.

207. Ralph L. Keeney, "Estimating Fatalities Induced by the Economic Costs of Regulations."

208. W. Kip Viscusi, "The Mortality Costs of Regulatory Expenditures: A Special Issue of the *Journal of Risk and Uncertainty*" (The Netherlands: Kluwer Academic Publishers, 1994).

209. Randall Lutter et al., "The Cost-Per-Life-Saved Cutoff for Safety-Enhancing Regulations," *Economic Inquiry* 37, no. 599 (1999): 608.

210. See ibid. See also Hahn, Lutter, and Viscusi, 16–17, for the scorecard. Using the scorecard, the authors conclude: "The majority of rules actually raise mortality risk on net at an income-mortality cutoff of $15 million, as figure 3-1 shows. At that cutoff, the total increase in mortality—among rules that increased mortality—was 230 expected deaths, although the reductions in mortality from a handful of rules swamped that. The total net reduction in mortality from all rules is 6,400. Thus, the full impact on mortality risk for all twenty-four regulations was beneficial." See also Keeney, "Estimating Fatalities Induced by the Economic Costs of Regulations."

211. There are a number of such studies. See Tengs and Graham, "Opportunity Costs," cited in note 23. See also R. H. Chapman et al., "A Comprehensive League Table of Cost-Utility Ratios and Sub-Table of 'Panel-Worthy' Studies," *Medical Decisionmaking* 20 (2000): 451–67. See, e.g., P. J. Neumann et al., "Preference-Based Measures in Economic Evaluation in Health Care," 587–611.

212. Morrall, "Saving Lives," 19. See section V in the present work for a discussion of the OMB's "prompt" letters, which promote regulations where benefits exceed costs.

213. See table 1, in section II, for an example of such a scorecard. A number of other examples related to RIAs and *Federal Register* notices present information on regulatory impacts. See, generally, Hahn et al., "Assessing Regulatory Impact Analyses," cited in note 85. See also Robert Hahn and Mary Beth Muething, "The Grand Experiment in Regulatory Reporting," *Administrative Law Review* 55 (2003): 607–42, available at http://www.aei-brookings.org/publications/abstract.php?pid=314. A similar line of research related to cost-effectiveness and public health is addressed in Neumann et al., "The Quality of Reporting in Published Cost-Utility Analyses," 1976–1997.

214. See Hahn et al., "Assessing Regulatory Impact Analyses," 868, cited in note 85: "Only 17 percent of the rules presented both a best estimate and a range of those quantitative benefits."

215. In this regard, it responds to one of the concerns raised by Parker about disregarding narrated benefits and costs. See also Robert W. Hahn and Patrick M. Dudley, "How Well Does the Government Do Cost-Benefit Analysis?" (2004), available at http://www.aei-brookings.org/publications/abstract.php?pid=418, assessing the quality of fifty-five regulatory impact analyses spanning three administrations.

216. A more detailed assessment could permit scoring on other dimensions that are more difficult to measure.

217. For examples of a case-study approach, see Richard D. Morgenstern, *Economic Analyses at EPA*, cited in note 92; and V. Kerry Smith, ed., *An Evaluation of Regulatory Impact Analyses* (Chapel Hill: University of North Carolina Press, 1984).

218. See Hahn and Muething, "The Grand Experiment in Regulatory Reporting," cited in note 213, providing a "scorecard" for how well the OMB report has met congressional objectives over the past six years and recommending ways that the government can produce better information on the benefits and costs of regulation. The authors recommend that the OMB require agencies to issue a scorecard evaluating each agency regulation, that the OMB summarize the strengths and weaknesses of regulations using this scorecard, that independent agencies be included in the OMB's analysis, and that Congress create an agency or office outside of the executive branch to perform a regulatory evaluation function similar to the OMB's.

219. See the *OMB 2003 Draft Report*, 5: "All of the estimates presented . . . are based on agency information or transparent modifications of agency information performed by OMB." The transparent modifications consist of annualizing agency numbers, converting to different year dollars, and

monetizing pollution reductions in a few instances where the agency does not monetize them.

220. Of course, if the oversight process resulted in substantial improvements in net benefits, then it could still be quite useful. In some cases, statutes may require a particular regulation, independent of whether it passes a cost-benefit test. For example, the Clean Air Act requires that the EPA set national ambient air quality standards for a variety of air pollutants, including ozone, but it allows some flexibility regarding implementation. Although regulations setting ozone standards have failed cost-benefit analyses—see *Report to Congress on the Costs and Benefits of Federal Regulation*, Office of Management and Budget (2000), table 13, available at http://www.whitehouse.gov/omb/inforeg/2000fedreg-report.pdf (hereinafter *OMB 2000 Report*)—the legislative mandate does not eliminate the need for oversight. Further analysis could still help develop a more cost-effective regulation.

221. See, for example, Heinzerling and Ackerman, *Pricing the Priceless*, 26: "[C]ost-benefit analysis also generally fails to achieve the goal of transparency. . . . Few members of the public can meaningfully participate in the debates about the use of particular regression analyses or discount rates which are central to the cost-benefit method." See also Shapiro and Glicksman, *Pragmatic Balance*, 96: "A better reform is to require that agency risk assessments be transparent. . . . These are pragmatic requirements because such transparency is a necessary foundation for two-way communication between government and the public it serves."

222. See Hahn, Government Numbers II, 87, n. 20: "Examples include a rule assessing the extent to which general federal actions conform to state or federal implementation plans under the Clean Air Act, a rule outlining the operating permits program of that act, and a rule describing data requirements for pesticide registration. The EPA only qualitatively described the benefits of those rules."

223. See Hahn and Sunstein, "A New Executive Order for Improving Federal Regulation: Deeper and Wider Cost-Benefit Analysis," table 4, for such a scorecard. See table 1 in the present work for a regulatory scorecard.

224. See *OMB 2003 Draft Report*, 5526, for an example of such a scorecard that the OMB advises agencies to complete for each regulation. This scorecard summarizes primary estimates and ranges for monetized, quantified, and qualitative costs and benefits.

225. See, e.g., Robert Crandall et al., *An Agenda for Federal Regulatory Reform*, AEI-Brookings Joint Center for Regulatory Studies, available at http://aei-brookings.org/admin/pdffiles/agenda_for_reg_reform.pdf: "Recommendation 8: Congress should experiment with a regulatory

budget for new regulations. Congress would set annual allowable limits for the regulatory costs imposed on society for different kinds of regulations, either by statute, by program, by agency, or for all regulatory agencies." See also Robert Hahn and Robert Litan, *Improving Regulatory Accountability* (AEI-Brookings Joint Center for Regulatory Studies, 1997) available at http://aei-brookings.org/admin/pdffiles/phpf4.pdf.

226. See, e.g., Hahn and Litan, *Improving Regulatory Accountability.*

227. See Eric Posner, "When Reforming Accounting, Don't Forget Regulation" (August 2002), available at http://www.aei-brookings.org/policy/page.php?id=104, introducing the concept of a "net benefit account" that would treat the benefits and costs of regulations as items on a balance sheet.

228. See, e.g., Hahn and Hird, "Costs and Benefits."

229. See, e.g., Harrington et al., "Regulatory Cost Estimates," undertaking a comprehensive comparison of more than two dozen ex-ante and ex-post cost estimates. The authors found that although per-unit cost estimates were broadly accurate, overestimation of aggregate costs was the norm. According to the authors, the likely implication of this finding is that over-estimation of aggregate benefits also appeared commonplace in these cases.

230. See Si Kyung Seong and John Mendeloff, *Assessing the Accuracy of OSHA's Projections of the Benefits of New Safety Standards*, 23, available at http://www.aei-brookings.org/publications/abstract.php?pid=357, cited in note 67, comparing ex-ante estimates of costs and benefits with ex-post estimates.

231. See Scott Farrow, "Improving Regulatory Performance: Does Executive Oversight Matter?" cited in note 93. My own work suggests that cost-effectiveness of regulations has become neither significantly better nor worse over time. Both works illustrate how the data initially developed by Morrall and others can be applied in different contexts. See also W. Kip Viscusi, *Risk by Choice: Regulating Health and Safety in the Workplace* (Cambridge, Mass.: Harvard University Press, 1983). See, e.g., Morrall, "Review of the Record."

232. Although any powerful tool can be manipulated for ideological purposes, the designer of the tool cannot always be held accountable for how the tool is used, since many applications exceed the scope of the designer's control. Similarly, I cannot always control how government and the public apply my scorecards. I can, however, suggest appropriate applications.

233. See Tengs and Graham, "Opportunity Costs," 171, 172, arguing that "some cost-ineffective interventions are fully implemented while other more cost-effective interventions are not. . . . How many lives could we save if we were to spend the same amount of money but invest it in those interventions that, taken together, would save the greatest number of lives possible?

Results indicate that if we hold investments constant at $21.4 billion and make funding decisions so as to maximize lives saved, we could save a total of 117,000 lives annually. That represents an additional 60,200 lives saved, or about twice as many lives relative to the status quo." See also Morrall, "Review of the Record."

234. See Freeman, "Environmental Policy since Earth Day I," 143, cited in note 194, suggesting that we can improve environmental policies by making them more cost-effective, using market-based incentives, giving more weight to cost-benefit comparisons, and "scaling back or eliminating specific regulations and standards where the costs per unit of measurable performance . . . are high and adopting more strict standards where costs per unit of performance are low." For a discussion on regulation and climate change, see William D. Nordhaus and Joseph Boyer, *Warming the World: Economic Models of Global Warming* (Cambridge, Mass.: The MIT Press, 2000). For a discussion of regulation of fine particles, see the EPA Clear Skies Act of 2003, available at http://www.epa.gov/air/clearskies/fact2003.html (accessed September 9, 2003). See also Cass Sunstein, "Consequences? A Response to Beyond Backyard Environmentalism," *Boston Review*, October/November, 1999: "Much of the national effort has shown poor priority-setting, with some small problems receiving disproportionate attention, and with some large problems being neglected. For example, government devotes excessive attention to the relatively small problem of abandoned hazardous waste sites, and far too little attention to the much larger problem of indoor air pollution."

235. See Paul R. Portney, "Economics and the Clear Air Act," 173, cited in note 195. See the discussion in section IV of the present work. See also Lutter and Gruenspecht, "Assessing Benefits of Ground-Level Ozone," cited in note 169.

236. Some critics raise concerns about the manipulation of scorecards. I think this is a red herring. The key point from my perspective is that scorecards can make and have made valuable contributions to our understanding of regulation.

237. This is precisely my view of their appropriate use.

238. Lisa Heinzerling and Frank Ackerman, *Pricing the Priceless*, 210: "The source of the problem is the atomistic and reductionist approach adopted in the dominant style of Cost-Benefit Analysis." For a concise review of *Pricing the Priceless*, see Cass Sunstein, "Your Money or Your Life?" *The New Republic*, March 15, 2004, available at http://www.powells.com/review/2004_03_11: "In the end, Ackerman and Heinzerling's argument seems to me to suffer from the authors' anachronistic and even Manichaean view of

the regulatory world. In their rendition, regulators can either stop evildoers from hurting people or prevent serious threats to human health and the environment. That is the right way to think about some environmental problems, to be sure—but most of the time environmental questions do not involve evildoers or sins. They involve complex questions about how to control risks that stem both from nature and from mostly beneficial products, such as automobiles, cell phones, household appliances, and electricity. In resolving those questions, we cannot rely entirely on cost-benefit analysis, but we will do a lot better, morally as well as practically, with it than without it."

239. Lisa Heinzerling and Frank Ackerman, *Pricing the Priceless*, 211: "Too much is lost in the atomistic approach." The basic argument is not new. See, e.g., Lester Lave, *The Strategy of Social Regulation*, cited in note 169. See also Lester Lave, "Benefit-Cost Analysis," cited in note 13: "We need to spend more time identifying attributes and must be more careful not to eliminate important attributes."

240. See Heinzerling and Ackerman, *Pricing the Priceless*, 211, 212: "The results do not necessarily agree with the public's desires. Indeed, the results often defy common sense, suggesting the public is willing to pay for almost nothing."

241. See Heinzerling and Ackerman, *Pricing the Priceless*, 212: "Much of the information used in an atomistic analysis would also be relevant in what we call the holistic approach, where costs as a whole (usually monetary) and benefits as a whole (often largely nonmonetary) are considered together—but are not forced to be expressed in the same units."

242. This is true, even though Heinzerling and Ackerman are careful to state, "Analysis of costs and benefits, in lowercase letters, is an essential part of any systematic thought about public policy, and has always been involved in government decision making." See *Pricing the Priceless*, 211. Although they agree that weighing costs and benefits is critical, they fail to acknowledge the specific advantages of cost-benefit analysis. See, for example, *Pricing the Priceless*, 200: "Thus we have come to the point where cost-benefit analysis no longer even possesses an internal logic." See also Arrow et al., "Benefit-Cost Principles."

243. Net benefits are typically defined as the difference between incremental benefits and incremental costs. Moreover, as is well known, virtually all measures of net benefits have problems because of the problem of making welfare comparisons across individuals. See, e.g., Kenneth Arrow, *Social Choice and Individual Values* (New York: Wiley & Sons, 1951).

244. See Cass Sunstein, *Risk and Reason*, for a discussion of the importance of cost-benefit analysis as a tool to identify ways of protecting health and extending lives that ordinary intuition would neglect.

245. See Environmental Protection Agency, *Arsenic in Drinking Water Rule: Economic Analysis* (Washington, D.C.: EPA, December 2000), 16, Exhibit 1-3, Net Benefits and Benefit-Cost Ratios of Each Regulatory Option. This table shows that net benefits are significantly negative at the most stringent arsenic standard considered, three micrograms per liter. See Heinzerling and Ackerman, *Pricing the Priceless*, 212, suggesting that the EPA's conclusion "that people would not be willing to pay the modest additional amount for the strictest possible level of arsenic regulation" defies common sense.

246. Ackerman and Heinzerling dispute the EPA's conclusion by using a different willingness-to-pay measure, prices of bottled water. Heinzerling and Ackerman, *Pricing the Priceless*, 214: "A holistic approach to the arsenic problem, for example, encourages us to ask whether it is worth the price of one or two bottles of water per person per year to ensure that everyone has tap water with the lowest possible level of arsenic. The atomistic approach sends us back to the mall to ask people about the monetary value of avoiding a nonfatal case of bladder cancer." See Environmental Protection Agency, *Arsenic in Drinking Water Rule*, section 1.4, for benefit assumptions: "The avoided premature fatalities were valued based on the VSL estimates."

247. There are many different views of how cost-benefit analysis should be implemented. See, e.g., Arrow et al., "Benefit-Cost Principles," 10: "Not all impacts of a decision can be quantified or expressed in dollar terms. Care should be taken to assure that quantitative factors do not dominate important qualitative factors in decisionmaking." See also Sunstein, *Risk and Reason*, 123: "Any cost-benefit analysis should include more than the monetary values by, for example, showing what the values are about, such as life-years saved and accidents averted. She [Heinzerling] may believe that many of the goods at stake in regulation (e.g., human and animal life and health, recreational and aesthetic opportunities) are not merely commodities, that people do not value these goods in the same way that they value cash, and that cost-benefit analysis, by its reductionism, is inconsistent with people's reflective judgements about the issues at stake. . . . But cost-benefit analysis should not be seen as embodying a reductionist account of the good, and much less as a suggestion that everything is simply a 'commodity' for human use."

248. See Lester Lave, *The Strategy of Social Regulation*, cited in note 169. See also Lester Lave, "Benefit-Cost Analysis," 127: "Many issues can be handled with simpler frameworks, such as 'no-risk,' 'technology-based standards,' or 'cost-effectiveness.'"

249. See Heinzerling and Ackerman, *Pricing the Priceless*, 214: "If the atomistic approach, valuing individual deaths, diseases, and environmental impacts, correctly analyzed the complete range of benefits, and if accurate, meaningful prices were available for all benefits, then the two methods would produce the same answer."

250. See Cass Sunstein, *Risk and Reason*, 108: "The risk that cost-benefit analysis will drown out relevant variables is not a reason to abandon the analysis, but to take steps to ensure against any such effect."

251. See Heinzerling and Ackerman, *Pricing the Priceless*, 8: "The basic problem with narrow economic analysis of health and environmental protection is that human life, health, and nature cannot be described meaningfully in monetary terms; they are priceless. When the question is whether to allow one person to hurt another, or to destroy a natural resource; when a life or a landscape cannot be replaced; when harms stretch out over decades or even generations; when outcomes are uncertain; when risks are shared or resources are used in common; when the people 'buying' harms have no relationship with people actually harmed—then we are in the realm of the priceless, where market values tell us little about the social values at stake." See also *Pricing the Priceless*, 207: "The imperatives of protecting human life, health, and the rich and poor, and of present and future generations, are not sold in markets and cannot be assigned meaningful prices."

252. See ibid., 213: "In short, a holistic assessment of one's options in the market leads to an either-or-choice: to buy or not to buy."

253. See ibid., 208–10: "An alternative method of decision making is badly needed. . . . [W]e do offer a set of principles for guiding public policy on life, health, and nature—principles that point toward a richer and more thoughtful way of making public policy in the new century. . . . Within this formal structure, what is the content of the alternative approach? What, in other words, should people push their representatives to do about health and environmental protection, in place of reliance on cost-benefit analysis? We propose four principles."

254. Depending on the weights you assign different principles, you could end up with different policy outcomes.

255. See Sunstein, *Risk and Reason*, 103: "In real-world controversies, a failure to regulate will run afoul of the precautionary principle because potential risks are involved. But regulation itself will cause potential risks, and hence run afoul of the precautionary principle too; and the same is true for every step in between. Hence the precautionary principle, taken for all that it is worth, is literally paralyzing. It bans every step, including inaction itself."

256. See Cass Sunstein, "Moral Heuristics," March 2003, available at http://papers.ssrn.com/sol3/papers.cfm?abstract_id=387941, for a discussion of how moral heuristics can lead to absurd moral judgments and systematic errors in risk regulation.

257. Of course, a decision maker could use these principles to make a decision, but the range of optimal outcomes using these criteria could be extraordinarily wide. This is true even when compared with an approach that maximizes net benefits subject to a constraint related to fairness.

258. See Heinzerling and Ackerman, *Pricing the Priceless*, 213: "To those who would respond that we are lost without a formula, we would point out, first, that many important decisions are made on the basis of rights and principles, not costs and benefits. . . . [M]ajor resource allocation decisions are repeatedly made, in the area of military spending and national security, with little or no concern for costs." But see Stephen Holmes and Cass Sunstein, *The Cost of Rights: Why Liberty Depends on Taxes* (New York: WW Norton and Company, 1999), for a discussion of balancing tests in "rights." Holmes and Sunstein argue that rights are not moral absolutes, independent of government constraints, but "public goods," funded by taxes, administered by the government, and subject to distributive justice. They maintain that no right is costless. Even rights are based on costs.

259. Indeed, examples of unsuccessful decisions where cost-benefit analysis was barred show how valuable cost-benefit analysis can be. For examples of regulations where costs exceeded benefits, see Freeman, "Environmental Policy since Earth Day I." Major regulations barred from cost-benefit balancing, such as the Federal Insecticide, Fungicide and Rodenticide Act, the Toxic Substances Control Act, and the Safe Drinking Water Act, were among Freeman's "losers," where costs exceeded benefits.

260. Cost-benefit analysis could, for example, illustrate the extent to which homeland security regulations constrain civil liberties. Although quantifying civil liberties is difficult, cost-benefit analysis could provide valuable insights in this area.

261. See Parker, "Grading the Government," 1413: "In principle, as seen above, rule- or project-specific cost-benefit analysis can meet these democratic and right-based concerns by detailing the impact of each regulation on the distribution of risk and loss, and by allowing ethical considerations to trump the numerical analysis wherever the physical or economic impact crosses a certain threshold." See also Shapiro and Glicksman, *Pragmatic Balance,* 79: "The fact that risk regulation produces aggregate net benefits, however, does not mean that individual regulations are not excessive or irrational. . . . [R]isk regulation makes a large positive contribution to

economic welfare in the aggregate. A more relevant consideration for policy purposes, however, is the impact of individual regulations."

262. See Freeman, "Environmental Policy since Earth Day I," 141, cited in note 194. Freeman cites Hamilton and Viscusi's 1999 study of 145 Superfund sites for which data are available. The mean cost per cancer case avoided is about $3.5 million. However, about 70 percent of the sites have estimated costs per case greater than $112 million. According to Freeman, these costs cannot be economically justified.

263. See George Stigler, "The Process and Progress of Economics," Nobel Memorial Lecture (December 8, 1982), 67: "The main reason for the considerable acceptance of the approach is that fundamental rule of scientific combat: it takes a theory to beat a theory. No amount of skepticism about the fertility of a theory can deter its use unless the skeptic can point to another route by which the scientific problem of regulation can be studied successfully."

264. I am not saying here that cost-benefit analysis should be the only factor informing the decision to pursue a policy. I am saying that, done well, it can serve as a very useful input in the decision-making process.

265. Parker supports rule- or project-specific cost-benefit analysis of regulations in principle, although he "does not take a position on cost-benefit analysis overall." See Parker, "Grading the Government," 1415. See Shapiro and Glicksman, *Pragmatic Balance*, 6, for qualified support of cost-benefit analysis: "[A]lthough regulatory analysis might inform us of the extent to which risk regulation is consistent with economic principles, it does not measure the extent to which risk regulation is consistent with the multiple social values that risk regulation serves. There is no mathematical, analytical tool to which one can turn for such an assessment. This does not mean that policy-makers and researchers should not perform such assessments, but it does mean that careful, qualitative analysis will be necessary." See Thomas O. McGarity, *Reinventing Rationality*, 125, advocating less ambitious varieties of regulatory analysis than cost-benefit analysis: "Although the theoretical limitations of formal cost-benefit analysis will probably prevent it from playing a large role in regulatory policymaking, less ambitious varieties of regulatory analysis can significantly improve regulatory decisionmaking if some of the practical impediments can be overcome."

266. For a more skeptical view on quantification, see Heinzerling and Ackerman, *Pricing the Priceless*, cited in note 53. See also the Center for Progressive Regulation website for its rejection of cost-benefit analysis, available at http://www.progressiveregulation.org/perspectives/costbenefit .cfm: "CPR believes that it is not useful to keep cost-benefit analysis around

as a kind of regulatory tag-along, providing information that regulators may find useful even if not decisive. Cost-benefit analysis is exceedingly time- and resource-intensive, and its flaws are so deep and so large that this time and these resources are wasted on it."

267. Parker, for example, would like to see a regulatory ombudsman. See Parker, "Grading the Government," 1420: "If the GAO does not fill the gap, the only clear, remaining alternative is to establish a new body to act as a sort of external 'ombudsman' in investigating allegations of regulatory fail- ure, reporting causes and recommending remedies." See also Parker, "Grading the Government," 1418, stating that "policy-makers and the pub- lic generally should defer to agencies in ambiguous cases, just as courts are already instructed to do."

268. See Stephen Breyer, *Breaking the Vicious Circle*, 11, discussing the problem of "tunnel vision" within agencies and defining tunnel vision in the regulation of health risks as "the last 10 percent" or "going the last mile." This happens when individual employees of an agency pursue a goal too far and enact regulation that imposes high costs without achieving significant additional benefits in an effort to clean up a substance that poses health risks.

269. See Arrow et al., "Benefit-Cost Principles," suggesting, as an improve- ment to the quality of economic analysis used in regulatory decision mak- ing: "Not all impacts of a decision can be quantified or expressed in dollar terms. Care should be taken to assure that quantitative factors do not dom- inate important qualitative factors in decisionmaking." See the discussion in section II.

270. See Arrow et al., "Benefit-Cost Principles": "[Q]uantify as many fac- tors as are reasonable and quantify or characterize the relevant uncertainties."

271. See Robert W. Hahn and Rohit Malik, "Is Regulation Good for You?" cited in note 147, for a more extensive discussion of unquantified benefits and costs.

272. Ackerman and Heinzerling state that, not only is cost-benefit analysis a "terrible way to make decisions about environmental protections," but it also "cannot simply be given some weight along with other factors" as a "kind of regulatory tag-along" (*Pricing the Priceless*, 33).

273. See, e.g., Crandall et al., *An Agenda for Federal Regulatory Reform*, cited in note 225, emphasizing that regulations should pass a broadly defined cost-benefit test.

274. See Stephen Breyer, *Breaking the Vicious Circle*, cited in note 5.

275. Heinzerling, however, does not seem to agree with quantifying uncer- tainty. See Heinzerling, Testimony before the Subcommittee on Energy

Policy, Natural Resources and Regulatory Affairs, 108th Cong., 2nd Sess. (March 2003), 8: "Another significant innovation in OMB's proposed guidelines is the requirement that agencies conduct a formal probabilistic analysis for rules with economic effects that exceed more than $1 billion per year. . . . This requirement adds significantly to the analytical burdens of agencies charged with protecting health, safety, and the environment."

276. For some insightful applications to the treatment of uncertainty, see, e.g., M. Granger Morgan and Max Henrion, *Uncertainty: A Guide to Dealing with Uncertainty in Quantitative Risk and Policy Analysis* (New York: Cambridge University Press, 1990). There is some debate about the use of point estimates to approximate the net benefits of regulations because of the large amount of uncertainty inherent in predicting costs and benefits. See, e.g., David Hassenzahl, "The Effect of Uncertainty on Cost-Effectiveness Estimation," *Journal of Risk Research* 8, no. 1 (forthcoming 2005), for an analysis of the importance of including information about uncertainty in regulatory decisions. In general, it is useful to consider uncertainties in key parameters. Unfortunately, regulatory impact analyses do not provide such information in a systematic fashion. In the absence of such information, I think point and midpoint estimates can provide some useful insights.

277. See Hahn et al., "Assessing Regulatory Impact Analyses," 868, cited in note 85.

278. See OMB, Best Practices I, section II.4: "Often risks, benefits, and costs are measured imperfectly because key parameters are not known precisely; instead, the economic analysis must rely upon statistical probability distributions for the values of parameters. Both the inherent lack of certainty about the consequences of a potential hazard (for example, the odds of contracting cancer) and the lack of complete knowledge about parameter values that define risk relationships (for example, the relationship between presence of a carcinogen in the food supply and the rate of absorption of the carcinogen) should be considered."

279. See *OMB 2003 Final Report*, 158: "Whenever possible, you should use appropriate statistical techniques to determine a probability distribution of the relevant outcomes. For rules that exceed the $1 billion annual threshold, a formal quantitative analysis of uncertainty is required."

280. McGarity argues for the importance of identifying "the winners and losers of a regulatory activity and the extent to which wealth shifts from one person to another." See McGarity, "Reinventing Rationality," 153. Noting that health and environmental regulations can have different impacts on people of different ages and on the rich versus the poor, he argues that regulators should pay attention to these distributional concerns. McGarity

cautions against accepting efficiency as the gold standard of regulation at the expense of other concerns such as distributional impacts.

281. See the discussion in section II.

282. The government would likely prefer to fund retrospective analyses that suggested that a regulatory decision had positive net benefits rather than negative net benefits. This could raise a problem with biases associated with government funding. The problem could be handled by having a research branch, such as the National Science Foundation, allocate the money, with the express intent of avoiding such bias. A more general problem is that many of the firms and researchers who could do this analysis receive substantial funding from the government. Peer review could also help limit bias in such cases.

283. The Office of Information and Regulatory Affairs, for example, has substantially improved the transparency of its regulatory oversight function by using the Internet more frequently to communicate information on regulations and regulatory impact analyses. See the OIRA website, at http://www.whitehouse.gov/omb/inforeg/regpol.html.

284. To improve transparency, the AEI-Brookings Joint Center is engaged in a project that would make old and new RIAs more easily accessible. By collecting, scanning, and posting the original RIAs to more than 250 regulations, the Joint Center aims to become a free online repository of agencies' economic analyses. For access to this repository, see http://aei-brookings.org/publications/index.php?menuid=3.

285. In this sense, I am in broad agreement with legal scholars such as Sunstein and Justice Breyer. Breyer identifies three problems that plague efforts to regulate small, but significant, health risks: tunnel vision, random agenda selection, and inconsistency. He believes that these problems warrant institutional change.

286. See Lisa Heinzerling, "Mythic Proportions," 2069: "It would be better, I think, if we left the picture blurry, and declined to connect the dots between all the confusing and sometimes conflicting intuitions and evidence." See Heinzerling and Ackerman, Pricing the Priceless, 33: "Nor is it useful to keep cost-benefit analysis around as a kind of regulatory tagalong." See, e.g., Shapiro and Glicksman, "Pragmatic Balance," 65: "The current system is better than a cost-benefit standard under conditions of bounded rationality."

287. See Robert W. Hahn and Robert Litan, "Recommendations for Improving Regulatory Accountability and Transparency," Testimony before the House Government Reform Committee, Subcommittee on Energy Policy, Natural Resources and Regulatory Affairs, 108th Cong., 2nd Sess.

(March 2003), 10, 12: "Congress should create a congressional office of regulatory analysis (CORA) or a separate agency outside of the executive branch to independently assess important regulatory activity occurring at *all* federal regulatory agencies. . . . As it is now, if and when Congress chooses to do so, it will have to rely on the agency's own estimates of the impacts of a rule and on any other data that interested parties may or may not have submitted in the rulemaking record."

288. See Parker, "Grading the Government," 1420: "[T]he only clear, remaining alternative is to establish a new body to act as a sort of external 'ombudsman' in investigating allegations of regulatory failure, reporting causes and recommending remedies." I would be delighted if Professor Sunstein would take the job, but there are several able social scientists who could also do a great job.

289. See Breyer, *Breaking the Vicious Circle*, 55–62.

290. OIRA issues prompt letters to the agencies to encourage them to issue regulations that are more cost effective and have higher net benefits. See Robert Hahn and Cass Sunstein, "Regulatory Oversight Takes Exciting New Tack," cited in note 63: "OIRA quietly announced a striking innovation: 'prompt letters,' designed to encourage agencies to explore new areas in which regulation might deliver benefits that exceed costs. . . . These 'prompt letters' are an exceedingly important development. For far too long, the idea of cost-benefit analysis has been wrongly associated with mindless opposition to regulation. To be sure, an exploration of costs and benefits often shows that regulation cannot be justified. But cost-benefit analyses can show, and have shown, that government action is worthwhile—and indeed that government should do more." For an example of a prompt letter, see http://www.whitehouse.gov/omb/inforeg/prompt_letter.html (accessed March 30, 2004).

291. See also Sunstein, *Risk and Reason*, 243, for a comparison of the costs and benefits of the EPA's ozone and particulates regulation: "If the EPA's conclusions are correct, the particulates regulation promises significant benefits, while the ozone regulation promises relatively small benefits at best." Sunstein also criticizes the EPA for not devoting enough of our limited public and private resources to the most serious problems, such as indoor air pollution, and spending too much on smaller pollution problems.

292. In contrast, the critics would probably be less sanguine about the use of return letters, which return a rule to an agency for reconsideration because of insufficient analysis or because costs exceed benefits. In my view, return letters serve a very useful function. They help to both make the regulatory process more transparent and highlight ways in which regulation

can be made more efficient. For examples of return letters, see the OMB's website at http://www.whitehouse.gov/omb/inforeg/return_letter.html (accessed March 30, 2004).

293. See section IV for a discussion of a regulatory budget.

294. See Eric Posner, "When Reforming Accounting, Don't Forget Regulation," cited in note 227, introducing the concept of a "net benefit account" that would treat the benefits and costs of regulations as items on a balance sheet.

295. Robin Hanson proposes making greater use of information markets for a broad array of policies. Michael Abramowicz offers specific suggestions on how such markets can be used to improve cost-benefit analysis. Robert Hahn and Paul Tetlock suggest how such an approach could improve the information base on costs and benefits, improve the efficiency of social regulations by paying for performance, and also address some of the problems associated with implementing a regulatory budget. See Robin Hanson, "Shall We Vote on Values, but Bet on Beliefs?" (2003, revised), available at http://hanson.gmu. edu/futarchy.pdf (accessed July 15, 2004). See, e.g., Michael Abramowicz, "Information Markets, Administrative Decisionmaking, and Predictive Cost-Benefit Analysis," *University of Chicago Law Review* 71, no. 3 (2004). See also Robert Hahn and Paul Tetlock, "Forecasting the Future: How Information Markets Could Change the Policy World," *Milken Institute Review* (forthcoming, 2005), available at http://www.aei-brookings.com/publications/ abstract.php?pid=815.

296. At a minimum, regulatory heads should not be precluded from explicitly weighing costs and benefits of policies as they are now in some cases. See Hahn, Government Numbers II, 54: "Numerous environmental, health, and safety statutes, such as the Occupational Safety and Health Act and most parts of the Clean Air Act, restrict the use of cost-benefit analysis in regulatory decisionmaking."

297. I think agencies should be permitted to use nonstandard values as well. Sunstein, for example, argues that the value of a statistical life should vary across different activities and people. See Cass Sunstein, "Are Poor People Worth Less than Rich People? Disaggregating the Value of Statistical Lives," available at http://www.aei-brookings.com/publications/abstract. php?pid=430. I agree in principle but am concerned about the potential for manipulation of results. In addition, I think it can be instructive to compare the effectiveness of different regulations using common measures that are transparent. Therefore, I would argue that agencies should be allowed to analyze benefits using different VSLs, but they should also be required to analyze regulations using a standard VSL to enable transparent comparisons across regulations.

298. I would actually go further and limit government involvement to areas where there are significant problems and a clear showing that the solution is likely to improve things.

299. See Parker, "Grading the Government," 73: "Indeed, think tanks produced two of the three shoddy studies this Article has critiqued."

300. Indeed, all studies I am aware of that deal with large amounts of data contain errors. See the discussion in section II.

301. I also believe that a significant fraction would pass such a test based on the government's numbers.

302. See Morrall, "Review of the Record," cited in note 17, for differences in cost-effectiveness across regulations.

303. Retrospective analyses may also suggest that different regulations pass and fail a cost-benefit test due to differences in implementation.

304. A larger group of RIAs would provide a more informed assessment. Also, much more work should be done on the issue of analytical quality. To date, the RIAs have been fairly difficult to acquire. Several agencies are now posting their RIAs routinely. The AEI-Brookings Joint Center embarked on a project to put as many final RIAs as we can find on the website, so scholars and interested observers of the regulatory process can access them more easily. See www.aei-brookings.org.

305. See Cass Sunstein, *Risk and Reason*, ix, suggesting that cost-benefit analysis should not be seen as a "form of cold, barely human calculation, treating life and health as mere commodities. . . . On the contrary, I urge that cost-benefit analysis should be seen as a simple, pragmatic tool, designed to promote a better appreciation of the consequences of regulation."

306. See Eric Posner, "When Reforming Accounting, Don't Forget Regulation," cited in note 227, arguing that the institution of net benefit accounts (NBAs) will promote more efficient regulations: "The well-run agency could build up a surplus in its NBA, allowing it to take risks with regulatory projects that might initially fail a cost-benefit analysis but, in the end, produce a net benefit for society."

307. See the discussion of benefits of environmental regulation in section IV. Interestingly, Parker does not critique my finding that the government's numbers reveal that there are substantial aggregate net benefits.

308. The problem with having regulators in agencies make decisions is that they tend to have "tunnel vision." See Stephen Breyer, *Breaking the Vicious Circle*, cited in note 5.

About the Author

Robert W. Hahn is cofounder and executive director of the AEI-Brookings Joint Center for Regulatory Studies and a resident scholar at the American Enterprise Institute. In addition, he is cofounder of the Community Preparatory School—an inner-city middle school in Providence, Rhode Island, that provides opportunities for disadvantaged youth to achieve their full potential.

JOINT CENTER